SIMPLE PLEASURES

CATS

Abyssinian

Siamese

American shorthair

British shorthair

Burmese

Birman

Manx

colourpoint

Scottish fold

longhair

CATS

MELITA KUNZ

With illustrations by Franco Testa

MICHAEL JOSEPH

For Elsa and Wolfgang

First published in Great Britain in 1989 by
Webb & Bower (Publishers) Limited,
9 Colleton Crescent, Exeter, Devon EX2 4BY,
in association with Michael Joseph Limited,
27 Wright's Lane, London W8 5TZ

Penguin Books Ltd, Registered Offices: Harmondsworth,
Middlesex, England
Penguin Books Australia Ltd, Ringwood, Victoria, Australia
Penguin Books Canada Ltd, 2801 John Street, Markham, Ontario,
Canada L3R 1D4
Penguin Books (NZ) Ltd, 182–190 Wairau Road, Auckland 10, New Zealand

Designed By Giorgio D'Andrea / Vic Giolitto
Series Editor Mariarosa Schiaffino
With illustrations by Franco Testa

Production by Nick Facer / Rob Kendrew

Translated from the Italian by Kerry Milis
Copyright © 1983 Idealibri SpA, Milan
Copyright © 1989 Idealibri SpA, Milan, for English translation

British Library Cataloguing in Publication Data

Kunz, Melita
Cats.
1. Cats
I. Title II. Series III. Il mondo e
gatto. *English*
636.8
ISBN 0–86350–263–6

Typeset in Great Britain by Scribes, Exeter, Devon

Printed and bound in Italy by Vallardi Industrie Grafiche

CONTENTS

INTRODUCTION
To the Altar and Back

S INCERE, faithful, sweet and affectionate . . . or false, hypocritical, faithless and self-centred?

For five thousand years, the cat has been accused of all of these, stirring up an ambiguous, confusing, contradictory polemic. But this has not always been the case. Both deified and burned at the stake, treated with affection and with insults, our diminutive hero has reached the threshold of the twenty-first century by making its way through temples, gutters, alleys, palaces, hovels, crusader ships and cat-show tables, surviving them all.

Meanwhile it has never betrayed itself by bartering intelligence or imagination for other more pressing needs. It has never worked as a sentinel or for the police or as a shepherd as dogs have, nor has it been a beast of burden or a companion at arms like the horse. It has not even been just a lovely background noise in the world of domestic intimacy, like the songbird in a cage.

Even when people have used it to catch rats and mice, the cat, far from being exploited or made to feel inferior, has turned the job into a game, a thing of pleasure, keeping complete control over its plan of attack.

Clearly you either love or you hate such a beast. There is no middle ground. And indeed, the cat has not passed through the centuries unnoticed. The footprints it has left behind have been indelible. The companion of both witches and saints, a symbol of the blackest betrayal and the fiercest independence, immortalized in paintings with Judas and the Madonna alike, sighed over in poetry and lacerated in prose, glorified in music and cruelly attacked in contemporary cartoons, for good or bad, the cat has captured the attention of kings, emperors, cardinals, people of genius and even Nobel prizewinners as well as the ordinary person.

Always regarded as 'different' because of its mysterious, almost extra-sensory powers, its fiercely anarchistic nature its complete lack of servility and the powerful feeling of sensuality it gives off, among the enlightened, the cat has come to be thought of as a precious friend one can draw on for power and virtue. For others, though, it is a scapegoat to be attacked with bloodthirsty hysteria.

A person is civilized to the extent that they understand cats, said Cocteau and rightly so. On the face of it, the highs and lows of cats throughout history have been a faithful reflection of civilization, a transparent image of human tolerance or of the abysmal stupidity of humanity.

The cat is a measure of our wisdom, in fact. Which is no mean feat.

CHAPTER I
THE ORIGINS OF THE CAT: SCIENCE, MYTH AND LEGEND

First, the Name

FROM hieroglyphics found in an Egyptian tomb around 2600BC, we read (if one can call it that) that our friend answered to the name of '*qato*'. This proved tenacious enough to stick through its future travels, staying with it even on its forced emigrations to Rome and Gaul.

Along the way *qato* became '*cattus*' in late Latin, '*katos*' in Greek, '*quett*' in Arabic, and in modern European langauges, '*gato*' in Spanish, '*katta*' in Swedish, '*katze*' in German, '*kat*' in Dutch and Danish, '*chat*' in French, and of course, 'cat' in English.

Some scholars, however, hold that the name comes from the Latin adjective '*cattus*' used to mean 'wise' or from the French verb 'guetter' (to spy).

The debate goes on, although I suspect there are few surprising revelations still to come.

Scientists Say . . .

. . . that fifty million years ago in the area called Eocene there lived an animal with a long body and short legs called 'miacid', the likely ancestor of the weasel, the cat and the dog. The miacid evolved into a number of different species and they eventually formed the great family of 'felidae'.

Its members all resembled each other and the biggest, brightest and most able of the breeds was the one that survived.

This was 'dinictis', a supercat about nine feet or nearly three metres tall (you should have seen it with the giant mammoths), with huge sabre-like teeth, an impressive muscular body and a rather small brain. Dog-lovers happily bring this up as a decisive argument in their favour in their on-going attack on cats (but what then should we make of humankind's own ancestry, which,

according to Darwin's theory of evolution, points back to the ape?).

But we will ignore them and go back to dinictis who, according to palaeontologists, appeared on earth about ten million years ago, long before any domestic or domesticable animal had arrived on the scene, in fact even before *Homo sapiens* was around to domesticate them.

When *Homo sapiens* did appear, it is rather curious (or perhaps not, knowing cats) that while there were signs of dogs, oxen and horses in their service, there is no sign of the cat . . . at least not in cave drawings.

A loner, free, a bit mangy and hungry but hardened and indomitable like the tired hero of many a western, it followed its antediluvian nature, battling with monsters much bigger than itself, while constantly sharpening its primordial hunting instincts.

It was not until around 3000 BC that the fierce isolationism of the cat was seriously but fortuitously attacked. A few dozen cats were captured by Sesostre, an Egyptian king and conqueror of Nubia, and thus they made their first appearance, in Egypt.

The days of glory had arrived and deification was just around the corner.

The Role of God

Knowing what an important role magic played in the lives of the Egyptians, it is not hard to imagine how certain physical characteristics of the cat and its behaviour must have struck them.

Cats' ability to see in almost complete darkness, thanks to the dilation and contraction of their pupils, was interpreted by the high priests of the time as an unequivocal sign of direct rapport with the sun.

Even when placidly curled up, purring away, the cat was believed to have a decisive link to the heavens, because this position resembled the lunar disk, symbolizing eternity. Soothsayers in their songs asserted that cats had the power to control the tides and influence atmospheric conditions and, thus, the growth of the crops.

Such supernatural powers of fecundity were seen as

divine and feminine. To take it one step farther and create an Egyptian goddess in the form of a cat was easy.

And when they chose, they chose well, creating Bastet, daughter of Isis, the goddess of the sun, the moon and the earth, and Osiris (also called Ra), god of the sun and the lower regions.

Clearly Bastet was born with the right connections. And she was given a special role, that of goddess of sexuality and fertility, along with the qualities and attributes of both her parents.

A human body with the head of a cat, wearing a long, often deep V-necked dress with elaborate embroidery, elegant and refined, this cat-goddess was worshipped for almost two thousand years in cults and ceremonies that frequently ended in extremes of ecstasy.

A typical example of the feasts in her honour was one held every year in Bubastis, ancient capital of Lower Egypt near the present day site of Tell Basta.

Here, around 950BC, King Osorkon II had a sumptuous palace built, whose magnificence was described by Herodotus:

> ... Other temples may have been larger or taller, but none was as stupendous as this one. Built completely out of blocks of red granite, it was in the shape of an enormous square or plaza, rising above the other buildings around it. On the other side of it, canals a hundred feet [thirty metres] wide brought water directly from the Nile and inside, in the centre, there was a little forest of low trees, protected by a little wall, which surrounded the altar of the goddess. The interior walls were richly decorated with inscriptions and many-coloured paintings. In one of them, showing King Osorkon II offering gifts to the cat-goddess, the inscription reads, 'To you I bow and offer all my lands. In you I recognize the powers of Ra'.

Returning to the feasts in honour of Bastet, from contemporary accounts they seem to have been an incredible success, and it is not difficult to see why.

Every year between April and May, more than 700,000 pilgrims arrived in Bubastis, filled with religious fervour and intense mystical enthusiasm, happy to be able to adore and worship their favourite god in such a pleasurable way.

Perhaps it was because of this that other accounts, more conservative or less pious, spoke of the festival as a kind of carnival of carnal delights.

Women devotees, arriving by boat, started undressing even before the boats pulled into shore, calling out greetings and bold remarks to the crowds waiting on the docks. Then off they went, dancing, singing and drinking wine through the streets, to the accompaniment of flutes and rattles. It must have been a short but auspicious step from collective delirium to orgy. Yes, I said 'auspicious' because for the governors of the region, such pleasure boded well for the fertility of fields, women, and animals alike. But this is no surprise. These were the very gifts of thanks and signs of benevolence that Bastet gave.

A Miniature Lion

Cats have always enjoyed the favour of those in high places where people's fate is decided.

If not always a god itself, at least the cat was created by a god, or so the ancient Greeks thought.

It is said that high on Mount Olympus, with all the disputes, vendettas and spiteful bickering of the gods, the handsome god Apollo decided to play a nasty trick on his brave and fearless sister Artemis (a dedicated huntress) by creating an animal so ferocious that all the other animals would submit to it and even his sister would be afraid. So he made the lion, future king of the jungle.

But, far from being frightened, Artemis thought it was a good joke and she decided to give Apollo a bit of his own back. So she designed an exact replica of his lion, but in miniature, and instead of a powerful roar, she gave it a strange small mewing sound.

It was a good lesson in doing things with a sense of measure and it was done with wit and style, two traits sadly lacking in that wrathful and vindictive bunch on Mount Olympus.

On Noah's Ark

After the Greek myths, came the Arab legends. Meanwhile, the Bible was strangely silent. The followers of Allah (who held the cat in great esteem), however, quickly filled the void.

According to one of their legends, among the animals who climbed up into Noah's Ark to take refuge from the floods was a pair of lively little mice. The nights were long on the Ark and the days were endless, filled with noisy chaos. And of course, it rained constantly. The boredom on board the boat was abysmal.

So the two little mice passed the time all snuggled up in a corner and . . . well, you can imagine what they did. The result was that there was soon an ever-increasing number of squeaky and very active little rodents who were becoming a serious threat to the food supply on board. Noah, who was a wise man, was forced to take drastic (and fantastic) measures. Going up to the lioness, he passed his hands over her head three times. She then sneezed and out popped (oh, miracle!) a cat. The problem of over-population in the rodent colony was solved, quietly and, may we say, ecologically, by today's standards.

A variation on this tale, again from the Arab world, has it that the king of the jungle simply grew bored during his long stay on the Ark. Now, the lion may have sleepy eyes but they hide a lusty nature behind them. One day, the lion forgot his royal responsibilities and practised his arts of seduction on a pretty young monkey in heat.

The result, a transgression of nature was – you guessed it – the cat. Which may explain, among other things, certain funny movements made in moments of greatest caprice.

CHAPTER II
THE CAT IN HISTORY

THE goddess Bastet may have monopolized the altars, but the Egyptian house cat (called '*mau*') also received its share of honour and glory as the fastest and bloodiest rat killer in the kingdom.

Egypt was the granary of the civilized world. Its enormous silos rivalled the pyramids in size but they also attracted hoards of voracious vermin who were a constant threat to the farms, isolated after each flooding of the Nile.

The cat saved the day by stopping the invasions at their source, thus helping Egypt to become the Kingdom of a Thousand Years.

Not surprisingly, the real reason according to some for the deification of the cat was as recompense for its feats in the war against the very real threat of rodents.

Whatever the reasons, the *mau* completely won the hearts of the Egyptian household. The care of the family cats was passed on from father to son and the death of a cat was a genuine tragedy for a household. The parents went into full mourning, shaving their eyebrows as a sign of grief and respect, and preparing elaborate funeral ceremonies.

The quality of the ceremony depended on the status of the cat in question. It has been calculated that a first-class funeral would have cost the equivalent of US$1,200 by today's standards while an ordinary one would have been about $200. Temple cats or cats from wealthy families were assured of immortality. They were first embalmed and then placed in special decorated caskets. It was not unusual to find mummies of rats buried along with them either as food or entertainment in the afterlife.

There were 300,000

In 1888 an entire cemetery of around 300,000 mummified cats was discovered in Beni Hassan, an area east of the Nile Delta not far from Bubastis. With no thought for their archaeological importance and no concern for even the most minimal cultural or religious sentiments the mummies were crammed into a merchant ship and sent off to Liverpool in England. There this precious cargo, weighing over twenty tons, was auctioned off as fertilizer at the rate of US$18 a ton. An account of the episode written at the time relates that during the auction the auctioneers even used the body of an embalmed cat as the traditional hammer. There have been no other discoveries quite like that one but the large number of mummified cats that still exists in Egyptian museums testifies to the richness and honour that the descendants of Bastet were accorded in death.

One of the mummified cats found by archaeologists in Egypt

As a kind of living god, such a valuable animal could never be exploited commercially. Smugglers received the death penalty: it was forbidden to take cats out of the land of the Pharaohs. Yet somehow around the first century AD, some Phoenicians managed to get away with it. Great businesspeople and able navigators, they secretly exported several pairs of cats lazing around the ports and let nature take its course. Soon they were able to sell the children and grandchildren of the stolen animals for high prices in Rome, Greece, Gaul and Britain.

Talisman of Conjugal Bliss

The weasel, which until then had been the Romans' favourite rat killer, was now replaced by the cat, who was such a good worker that it earned the title of '*genius loci*'.

As the divine protector of the house its blessing was invoked when a marriage took place. Once the young wife was in possession of the new home she would offer a sacrifice and a symbolic contribution of money.

This concept of the cat as a protective presence in the home spread throughout Europe. In Flanders, during the Middle Ages, for example, if a white cat was found on the doorstep of the new home before the marriage it was a sign of certain happiness. Conversely, an old French proverb advised any young girl who had stepped on the tail of a black cat not to marry for at least a year. During the same period, it was customary in Scotland to celebrate the arrival of a new cat with a special ritual: the animal was carried around the hearth three times and then its paws were rubbed against the fireplace. It was believed that this would keep the cat from running away, taking with it the family's domestic happiness.

A cruel Scandinavian custom signalled the beginning of a tragic period in the history of our friends. To ensure good luck, farmers walled up a live cat inside the foundations of a new building so that its spirit would protect them from natural calamities. There have been reports of this same custom in England. During the restoration of the Tower of London, for example, construction workers uncovered a series of cats walled up in a wing of the ground floor.

The Dark Medieval Times

Although the words and example of Saint Francis helped create a feeling of love and benevolence towards animals in the thirteenth century it was not enough to save kitty from the furious hysteria of the Inquisition.

Books have been written about the reasons for this unexpected aboutface towards 'the harmless and helpful cat' as Shakespeare called it, who now became an emissary of the devil.

The one thing that is certain is that it took the Black Death in the fourteenth century to harden hatred towards the cat, who was now judged just as mercilessly for its past as for its present. Had not this representative of the cat family been deified in Egypt by pagans and venerated by infidels? Had not a cat been a symbol for Freya, goddess of orgiastic rituals? And worst of all, was the cat not a companion and aid to witches as they invoked the name of Satan on their Black Sabbaths?

In an era when the Church feared idolatry above all else, the cat reeked of the odour of divine wrath.

It was not enough simply to ridicule cats or even just to keep away from the poor animals. They had to be fiercely and publicly pursued.

In October 1347, some Italian ships from Genoa landed in the port of Messina on Sicily. On board were dead and dying men all showing the same symptoms: swollen rotting pustules on their bodies that broke open, signalling an imminent death. It was the plague, the fourth horseman of the Apocalypse.

The plague had already been around for several centuries, accompanying the raids of Huns and Ostrogoths and even the devout Crusaders returned home in ships laden both with glory and pestilent Asian rodents. And yet the wrath of God had never struck with such virulence as in the fourteenth century, raising doubts about the very survival of Western civilization.

Contemporary accounts saw it as the end of the world which was a pardonable exaggeration. Most historians now agree that three out of four people in Europe died, and twenty-five million lives were cut short.

There was not a city, village or country, not a palace, hovel or convent that was spared the sharp sickle of the Black Death. Everywhere there was weeping and mourning and the total ignorance of its cause only increased the sense of horror and general feeling of helplessness.

No one had any idea that the carriers of this dreadful disease were two very familiar and domestic little animals, the rat and its fleas.

Instead, people turned to the infectious swamps and unhealthy villages, the sulphurous vapours released by earthquakes. There were even some who believed that the planets and oceans were engaged in a titanic struggle caused by the Devil. In any case both medical and public belief were obsessed with the theory of evil astral influences, the *longa manus* of divine punishment.

Unable to do anything and unwilling to become, like some, bloodied and penitent flagellants (who anyway died like everyone else), many people focused their attention on three categories of 'foreigners' judged to be the cause of this evil: Jews, witches and cats.

The first, as the eternal outsiders, were accused of poisoning the water in wells to 'destroy Christianity and rule the world' (an accusation going back to the Athenian plague when it was used against the Spartans!).

There was also no need to invent excuses for blaming witches – they were judged guilty for the strange company they kept, their blasphemous rituals and their occult practices, and publicly burned at the stake.

(Today these same victims of popular furor are called fortune-tellers, prophets, mediums, clairvoyants and astrologers. They write books, publish magazines, appear on television and even advise presidents. Every December they keep everyone in suspense as they make their predictions for the coming New Year.)

The third party accused without defence in those dark and sinister times was the cat, the *alter ego* of the witch and her faithful companion in witchcraft – except when it was up to worse mischief . . .

The Cat as Scapegoat

According to contemporary accounts of trials (some of which are reported in a book called *Malleus Malefi-carum*), many witches spontaneously 'confessed' to having had intimate relations with Beelzebub who had taken on the earthly form of a monstrous black cat. Others confessed to having nursed or fed him by night with their own blood.

Sexual partner or son of the devil, the cat continued to be a repository of the darkest secrets of black magic, the earthly and evil form of the souls of the damned wandering over the earth.

Purification by fire was the only way to destroy them. And so the slaughter of the innocents began.

A particularly memorable one was in France, in Metz, originally started to clean up a clearly satanically inspired epidemic of St Vitus's dance, and repeated for hundreds of years. Another notable one took place in Ypres, a Flemish village noted (up until the Second World War) for its custom of throwing off one of its towers all the cats captured in the vicinity on the first Wednesday of August every year. Another, the Taighern, stands out for its long duration, four days and four nights happily grilling Teutonic cats, with the prize of 'second sight' to the one who roasted the most. Finally, the best of them all. On St John's Eve in Aix en Provence cats were consumed in a big bonfire as part of the general celebrations.

In all these rituals, of clearly pagan and pre-Christian origin, sacrifices were made to the Devil, but it was not unheard of for the object of veneration to be God himself.

This happened, for example, during the celebration of the coronation of Elizabeth I, queen and head of the Anglican Church. A special wicker basket carrying an effigy of the detested Pope was stuffed with live cats, carried through the streets of London followed by a cheering crowds, and burned in front of Westminster Abbey. It was said that the cries of the dying cats were the cries of devils coming from the body of the Holy Father and that God was very pleased with this 'burning' and condemnation of the heretical Church of Rome.

The religious hysteria of the masses that reached such

extremes in those days (which unfortunately lasted almost four hundred years!) seems improbable today.

A typical case was that of a Scottish merchant who claimed that each day part of his wine supply was soured and part had disappeared. He told the courts that he had hidden in his storerooms to catch the thief in the act, and found menacing black cats *in loco*. He wounded one gravely with a sword and the following day he discovered a farmer in the vicinity, already suspected of witchcraft, with a noticeable limp from an ugly cut on his leg. This was enough to send the unfortunate fellow to the stake.

Youngsters torturing two cats and throwing them into a well.
The drawing is by William Hogarth.

That witches could transform themselves into cats was an accepted fact, especially after many witches (always under torture) confessed to it, using the magic words: 'The Devil speed thee and go thou with me.'

This particular type of transformation was the subject of many learned studies, to the extent that in 1584 a book called *Beware the Cat* by John Baldwin tried to establish once and for all that a witch could not assume the form of a cat more than nine times.

This reference to the nine lives of a cat came about in this period as a direct extension of the Threefold Laws of Witchcraft, which said that good or bad practised with witchcraft comes back threefold on the person who practises it. The cat as an emissary of Satan had the honour of seeing that diabolical power not just trebled but cubed.

On the same subject but with a very different spirit and sense of humour Mark Twain, a few centuries later, said, 'One of the most important differences between a cat and a lie is that the cat only has nine lives.'

Things Finally Change

The terrible plague that had raged through London had killed half the population. But time had not gone by completely in vain and the idea of the usefulness of the cat in these difficult times was beginning to make headway. The Church revised some of its ideas about their merits, even going so far as to say in the *Ancren Riwle* that the cat was the only animal to be allowed in convents and monasteries.

The ardent cat killers had also lost power in France under the reign of Louis XIV.

Richelieu left a large part of his will to fourteen cats who shared his life and often partook of the honours and functions of his high office. In his famous fairy tale, Perrault portrayed the traits of loyalty, imagination and cleverness with a cat in a pair of boots which dedicated itself exclusively to the happiness of its owner.

However it was the Enlightenment that finally brought an end to the madness of the previous persecutions, and the French Revolution completed the work by sweeping away almost all the tenacious residue of cat phobia. But superstitions and deep-rooted antipathies die a slow death. In the same period, for every Chateaubriand who highlighted feline virtues in his *Mémoires d'outre tombe* there was a Napoleon who had a violent attack of nerves if he saw a cat shortly before a battle.

Meanwhile on the other side of the Atlantic in America our hero was proving itself very useful in the new colonies against the invasions by hungry hordes of rats.

News of this new victory of the cat spread throughout Europe. Decisive confirmation of its value came when cats slaughtered the source of the plague that hit Napoleon's troops in 1799 during an expedition to Egypt.

Once again an agent of good, even if no longer a god, the cat had repelled the last prejudices that held on here and there – but it would not become a household pet until the nineteenth century.

The Year of Redemption

It is said that the Victorian era was the *belle époque* of the cat and certainly, compared with previous ones, it contributed a great deal to giving them back their dignity and social standing.

This was in part thanks to Louis Pasteur. The scrupulous hygiene that he imposed as he went about his scientific discoveries revealed how unpleasant were some of the habits of humankind's traditional best friend and placed the cat in a new light. Finally, the cat was seen with fresh eyes, first as a clean, useful animal and then as a beautiful and exotically refined one.

Greatly admired in drawing rooms of the period for example were a pair of cats given by the king of Siam to the English consul in Bangkok and sent by them back to England with full honours. Another important step was the publication of *The Cat, its History and Diseases* by the Honourable Lady Cust (Lady Mary Anne Boode), the first book (thirty-one pages) on the care of cats. Though the first edition of 1856 was received with scepticism and irony, it was followed by another in 1870 that enjoyed a huge success. The times were ripe for the event that followed the next year, the glorious resurrection of the cat via the first cat show at the Crystal Palace in London.

CHAPTER III

FROM THE CRYSTAL PALACE TO THE EMPIRE CAT SHOW

Almost a New Ascot

'WHEN the day arrived for awarding prizes, I bought a ticket and took the train to the Crystal Palace, leaving from Ludgate Station. I have to confess that while sitting there completely alone on a comfortable upholstered seat in a first class carriage, I was terribly anxious about the success of my experiment. There was no way I could have imagined the scene that would soon present itself before my eyes. Everything was so new! . . .

While I was deep in thought, the door of my carriage opened and an old friend of mine entered. "How are you?" he asked. "I'm well," I replied. "I'm on my way to a cat show." "Where!?" exclaimed my friend, and added, "Well, that takes the cake! A cat show! I loathe cats. If I catch one around my house, he's out in a second."

"I'm sorry you don't like cats," I replied. "I, for my part, admire their beauty and their graceful movements and the fact that they are so domestic, quite often more so than dogs; they are also good rat catchers. Furthermore, they can do things like jump on a door handle and push it down with their paws, and they can tell Sunday from the rest of the week to the extent that it is the one day they don't wait for the man who brings the meat to come by."

"That's enough," rebuked my friend. "You may like cats, but I don't. I don't want to discuss it further." "Not so fast," I responded. "That is the very reason I have organized this show, because I want the world to see how beautiful a well cared for cat is, as sweet and gentle as a lamb. Come with me to the show, my friend, and you won't be sorry."

So it was that my friend and I entered the Crystal Palace together. The cats were in their cages, lying on beautiful damask cushions . . . Here and there you could hear purring . . . Cats of the most varied colours and

markings, together with gorgeous white Persians.

As we passed by the pens, I noticed that my friend was growing more interested. It wasn't long before he broke out with a "There's a real beauty!" and "Look at that one over there . . . I had no idea there were so many different kinds and colours and sizes!"

A few months went by and I paid a visit to my friend. I found him having breakfast and by his side in a chair, sat two well behaved cats. All three, companions, by the look of it.'

The author of the account above was Harrison Weir, an eccentric, an artist and clearly a passionate cat-lover. In that first cat show sponsored by him in 1871, he exhibited almost two hundred cats for the curious. Among others, there was a famous pair of Siamese, recently arrived from Bangkok, a French-African cat with very soft brown fur, a splendid grey cat just arrived from Persia and an enormous native cat with the more than respectable weight of 21 pounds (9½ kilos) who won the prize for 'Fattest Cat'.

The show was a huge success and became an annual event. Thanks to visits by the royal family and the acquisition of two magnificent cats by Queen Victoria, it also became very fashionable.

In a few years, the Crystal Palace Show became an important occasion on the London social calendar, an event not to be missed. In 1889, there were more than 600 noble cats shown. More than 20,000 people meandered through the show to admire the furry beauties and perhaps to dream of owning one that they could fawn over and display like a work of art.

For centuries people have been raising cats, but I've never met anyone who has studied them seriously.

This statement by the abbot Galiani, a brilliant economist and sharp wit of the eighteenth century, was given the lie nearly one century later by an outburst of books and scientific treatises on cats.

One of the first naturalists to do so was John Pocock (1863–1947). Leaving aside the *Felis silvestris* or wild cat and beginning instead with the *Felis domesticus* that we call the tabby, Pocock undertook an in-depth study of

Some of the cats at the Crystal Palace Show, from a
period drawing

all the known kinds of cats, arriving at a precise classification of the different types which was used by cat shows from 1925 onwards. Until that time cats who were exhibited were judged on their appearance only. But from 1925 on, precise definitions were set up by the National Cat Club of London which defined the characteristics of the different breeds based on biological and genetic differences.

A Qualitative Leap

Since then, over time, new classifications have been added to those early ones. Today American and British cat federations recognize thirty-three different breeds, besides numerous variations obtained over the years from experiments in cross-breeding.

The net results of these experiments in breeding have reached the hundreds. This seems almost like science fiction for those whose only idea of a 'fancy' cat is the Persian (inevitably confused with the Angora) and who think of the ordinary shorthaired cat as being like the big tiger-striped tom belonging to the old lady next door, the milkman's ginger cat, the neighbour's black and white one, or the scruffy half-starving black ones down by the docks. None of these, of course, has a pedigree. Yet there is a difference between British and American shorthairs.

A standard has been established by the Governing Council of the Cat Fancy, a British organization, which some time ago decided to legitimize the shorthair, defining two different breeds, the British and the American, who then had the right to enter even the most prestigious cat show.

So the gypsy life of the street cat, making its way through back alleys and rooftops, ended and the era of judging began. It may not have been divine or universally accepted, but at least it was done by an élite circle of cat experts of international rank.

Those were the days . . .

'In my day the shows were . . . how shall I say it . . . well attended. Not only were the cats . . . aristocrats but also the visitors . . . you know what I mean . . . A certain elegance, a style, a tone was set . . . believe me, you cannot imagine. Yes, there is a lot of publicity in the newspapers today and the public goes and they all want to know and observe and they ask questions . . . I don't deny that . . . That's fine for general knowledge and the improvement of the breeds. But tell me the truth: just look around you . . . Do you see the kind of people they are and how they dress?'

The person speaking is an elderly upper-crust lady who followed cat shows for fifty years with a true passion. Her nostalgic memories echo those of many people of her age who miss the order, the composure, the distinction of the past and in her case the gold frames of the cages added a certain lustre as well.

As for those 'people', it is not really as if they were dressed to go to Carnival in Rio . . .

Chronicle of a Cat Show

Today, visitors to a cat show are a cheerful, noisy crowd full of goodwill and curiosity, loving couples, groups of teenagers, bearded intellectuals, children running all over the place with grandparents chasing after them, and the odd dowager in hat and sensible shoes . . . Everyone is chattering away, staring, pushing, using words lilke 'teeny' and 'dear little . . .' and sticking their fingers in the cages to touch whatever they can, even if it is just a hair of those royal furs.

Meanwhile, what are the champions, the divas, doing?

Lying in cells lined with damask and velvet, with lace curtains and little bows, they are disdainful and showy. Drowsy, bored and indolent, their minds on other things, some hide under silk cushions, others turn their backs on the crowds, yawning and stretching. None of them condescends to look at the brimming bowls full of tempting titbits, as if their appetites were forever sated.

What has become of the cat-cats that we know and love, the vigilent, attentive, roguish and tender, sweet and disdainful, playful gluttons?

In an atmosphere where apathy reigns supreme, the greatest amusement perhaps comes from reading the suggestive and high-flown names of these precious furry mummies in the catalogue.

A reflection of the whims of their owners, their noble titles overflow the pages where we find, for example, a Joster von Schloss Aarburg, a Kalif du Petit Manoir, a Zarina Heures Bleues, a Countess Chantal de Dignatic, an Electra degli Scaligera and a Shanida de Rocheblonde.

The democratic United States also serves as a source of inspiration, but this time the names are less pretentious and more adventurous, such as Gringo of Arizona, Eldorado or The Bandit of the Big Dipper. And for the beautiful star-cats, what more appropriate name than Circe of Bahia, Marlu Messalina, Madame Pompadour, Babarella or Elixir of Love, evoking their voluptuously sensual charms.

In the midst of a medley of ribbons, trophies and awards, through a cloud of talcum powder, sprays and perfumes, and piles of brushes, combs, jewelled collars and other symbols of affection, through the roaring confusion of background noise, only interrupted by loudspeakers calling judges and vets to the scene, the show goes on.

In Britain there are over ninety shows during a show season (the show year begins in June and ends the following May) and seventy-five of them are considered Championship shows. Two of the largest are the National Cat Club's and the Midland Counties Cat Club shows. The Governing Council of the Cat Fancy holds one, the Supreme, which is equivalent to Crufts in the dog world.

In the United States, there are eight registering bodies, each with a number of associated clubs, with the biggest being the Cat Fanciers' Association. A cat can be registered with more than one of these cat assocations and thereby be exhibited at many local cat shows. These are usually one- to two-day shows and the most famous one is the Empire Cat Show held each year in Madison Square Garden in New York.

Those interested in attending a cat show in their region should write for information about the nearest one to the Governing Council of the Cat Fancy in England (4–6 Penel Orlieu, Bridgwater, Somerset TA6 3PG) or the Cat Fanciers' Association in America (PO Box 203, Port Lookout, MO 65726).

CHAPTER IV

THE USEFULNESS OF CATS

> When rats infest the palace, the slowest
> cat is better than the fastest horse.
>
> *Old Japanese proverb*

THROUGHOUT history, cats have undoubtedly been best known as rat catchers, both in the East and the West.

In AD999, the Japanese emperor Ichijo found five newborn kittens in a corner of his palace in Kyoto. Because they were born on the tenth day of the fifth moon, a very sacred time, the emperor ordered that they be protected and given the best of care and attention.

From that point on, the Japanese cat enjoyed centuries of luxury and idleness, until sometime between the thirteenth and fifteenth century, when it was discovered that it could be used to protect silkworms from rats. The court was so convinced of the cat's magical powers of deterrence that the emperor had stone effigies of cats made and placed in all the so-called 'warm' spots, such as the kitchen, granary, and hay loft, to scare the rats away.

Eastern exploitation of the cat reached its peak in 1961. That year, hundreds of cats were carrried off from the back alleys of Singapore's port area and dropped by parachute into the rat-infested rice paddies of Borneo to save the harvest.

A Domestic Barometer

The city cat living in an apartment has few possibilities these days to demonstrate its skill as a rat catcher (fortunately for us). But it does serve another useful function – as a barometer.

In France and Italy, for example, a cat scratching behind its ear with its foot means it will rain, or at least that the weather will get worse. In China, the same meaning is attributed to it winking its eyes; in Scotland, to it rubbing against the legs of a table; and in Denmark, to it running madly up and down the stairs for no appa-

rent reason. It is as if the cat can 'feel' the weather.

Certainly, such sensitivity has been extremely useful for sailors, who (rats in the hold apart) have always held cats in high esteem.

Even today, if a Greek sailor throws a cat into the sea it is thought to bring on a storm. In the same vein, until the end of the last century a curious ceremony was often carried out on the bridge of a suddenly becalmed ship using our hero as an intermediary to the god Aeolus to bring on favourable winds.

As at sea, so in the countryside. Favourable winds and good fishing for the sailor, a warm sun and a good harvest for the farmer. The cat was important to both, communicating with the heavens to bring a cornucopia.

In Sweden, for instance, back in the mists of time, farmers would leave big crocks of fresh milk outside their doors for the four grey cats that pulled the chariot of Freya, the Norse goddess of love and fertility.

Old habits die hard and this is even more true of superstitions and fantasies, especially those regarding cats and their dual natures of good and evil.

In many regions of Europe, while the children were careful not to trample the young wheat growing in the fields for fear of being devoured by the awesome phantom cat of the fields, harvesters accidentally cut with a scythe immediately looked for an obliging cat to lick their wounds. Otherwise they risked losing the harvest.

In Briançon in France, at the beginning of the harvest, neighbourhood cats were actually festooned with garlands of flowers and ribbons and only when the harvest was over was their uncomfortable embellishment removed.

In other regions of France, the last sheaf to be gathered together and tied was called the 'cat's tail' and the peasant who had gathered it put it over their shoulder and, grabbing the partner of their choice along with a bundle of corn ears, chased the others in a kind of game of tag to bring good luck to the earth and to the bread-making to come.

A Good-luck God

Except for the continuous misadventures of the dark ages and those incidents arising from superstition (unfortunately not limited to the past), the cat has always been seen as a good-luck charm.

I have already mentioned some of the qualities attributed to our sphinx of the hearth and domestic talisman. The prize for the firmest believers in this respect however must go to the ancient Egyptians. This is hardly suprising, given their passion for the afterlife and for all kinds of amulets.

One very popular custom among Egyptian newlyweds was that of exchanging a pendant of enamelled ceramic, coloured either blue or green, in the shape of a mother cat feeding her young. The newly married couple firmly believed that the number of kittens on the figure would be the same number of children that their home would eventually be blessed with.

And that is not all. The cat-goddess Bastet who was the source of happiness and good health, was often represented on an eye-shaped amulet called a *'utchat'*.

The Egyptians were firm believers in these pendants and attributed to them the power to protect them from death, illness and unlucky occurrences. Similar to the various charms still used in southern Italy today, these were used to decorate houses and embellish tombs, and

The cat is a common Oriental symbol of good luck.
This one is Chinese.

were also worn around the neck and wrists or attached
to pins as if they were precious jewels.

One of the most common ones had a number of small
cats filling the space between the eye and the pupil of
the *utchat*. If the name of Bastet was inscribed on the
back, its power against calamity was even greater.

In Britain of course, the black cat has always been and
still is the good-luck symbol *par excellence*, and in the
Far East also cats continue to be used in good-luck
charms.

One is the '*maneki-neko*' (literally 'the inviting cat'),
which has become a symbol in Japan for prosperity.
Placed at the entrance of restaurants and businesses, a
cat with one paw raised up to its ear in a kind of greeting,
the *maneki-neko*, by using its influence, is believed to
attract customers and to guarantee good business (in
keeping with this, the other paw often holds a gold coin).

In another example, which in fact is rather cruel,
merchants keep one or two cats collared and chained to
their counters. The older the cat (and therefore the
longer it has spent chained there), the greater its owner's
profits are supposed to be – or at least so these businesspeople think.

Kitty goes to War

Another jump backwards in time and we are once again
in Ancient Egypt, around 525 BC, when a famous episode
occurred whereby cat 'soldiers' intervened directly in the
military history of a country.

The incident took place during the long siege of
Pelusium, an Egyptian city near present-day Port Said.
Here the Persians had tried for months to break the

fierce resistance of the Egyptians, who were led by Psamtik III. Though they had tried everything, it had been in vain and finally there was nothing for them to do but retreat.

Then suddenly at the last minute Cambyses II, the son of Cyrus the Great, had a brilliant idea. He gave orders to his troops to leave the site undefended and sent his strongest soldier off to collect every cat he could find in the city and surrounding countryside. His booty was even better than hoped for, and the next morning, fortified with this extraordinary contingent, Cambyses released some of the cats on to the battlefields. The rest he had strapped to the arms of his shield bearers and these he sent to advance on their enemies.

A cat used during war, from a sixteenth-century engraving

Today a Mel-Brooks-like scene such as this would make us die with laughter, but then it created an unimaginable uproar among the Egyptians. So great was their horror of sacrilege that they put down their lances and arrows for fear of wounding even a single cat.

The defeat was disastrous, Pelusium became Persian and, as a constant reminder of the event, a temple to Zeus Cassius was erected, the remains of which can still be seen today in Tell Farana.

But even though this example of the cat as warrior remains unique, legends and superstitions of another type have persisted throughout the centuries showing another way the cat has been useful, one we might call para-pharmaceutical.

The Four-legged Panacea

In ancient Rome, Pliny maintained that cat excrement mixed with mustard could cure ulcerous head wounds, while for lacerations of the uterus he recommended the same base product mixed with resin and rose oils.

Like the Egyptians and their *utchat*, the Celts fell in love with the eyes of the cat, above all for the singular quality of their irridescent pupils, reduced by day to a narrow opening, dilated and phosphorescent at night, and even capable of producing a mild hypnotic effect in certain people.

In many Celtic legends, the cat's eye is a window into the palace of the fairies, a tiny crack open to whomever wants to look into a magic kaleidoscopic world full of fantasy. Unfortunately, however, the observation that the iris of a calm tranquil cat transmits the same pleasurable relaxation in the person looking at it, produced not only wonderful fairy tales but also more than a few deviations and distortions.

The pupils of our poor friends became the main ingredient in a series of potions and nasty mixtures to cure all sorts of maladies, from blindness to hysteria, from lovesickness to melancholy.

Naturally, the only ones to be persecuted for using them were those presumed to be witches who were thought to enjoy the help of Satan in making the potions. For other people, there were still plenty of quacks and pharmacists, pseudo-scientists and experts in bloodletting, purifications and distillations to help cure them of their ills.

Frequent use was also made of dessicated cat's liver, even as late as the 1700s when Edmund Topsell in his *Histories of Foure-Footed Beastes and Serpentes* recalls its beneficial use in bladder problems.

The cat's tail could also be used for treating things like scabies, nettlerash, and epilepsy. Even for getting rid of warts, as Huckleberry Finn says in *Tom Sawyer*:

> . . . you take your cat and go and get in the graveyard 'long before midnight when somebody that was wicked has been buried; and when it's midnight a devil will come . . . you heave your cat after 'em and say, 'Devil follow corpse, cat follow devil, warts follow cat, I'm done with ye!'

Life Insurance

Today doctors still consider cats a useful therapy for the care of our bodies and souls, though in a somewhat different way.

Research and computer data have established beyond a shadow of a doubt that people who live with cats have a 33 per cent higher life expectancy than average (for dog owners the percentage drops to 20 per cent). There are many reasons for this. For example, talking to a cat the way it likes to be talked to, that is, calmly, tenderly and quietly (never irritably), caring for it and feeding it, helps to maintain the neurological system on an even keel, to keep blood pressure down and to avoid the spectre of a heart attack.

For the elderly person living alone, having a four-legged beast to care for, with defined needs (food, shelter and affection) can drive away loneliness, depression and the feelings of uselessness that are so often fatal after a certain age. Why do cats beat dogs by a full 10 per cent when it comes to helping people live longer? Those indispensable daily walks which our traditional best friend requires can be a real source of calamity – bringing chills, sprained muscles and attacks of arthritis.

In America, this use of cats has been recognized for some time and many associations now give away one or two cats to old-age pensioners who live alone, in the hope among other things that this will lower their consumption of medicines and thus one of the community's expenses. In the United Kingdom, the Society for Companion Animal Studies in conjuction with the British Small Animal Veterinary Association has drawn up guidelines for introducing pets into such institutions as old people's homes, believing that being around a pet can raise people's morale and their sense of self-esteem and make them feel more cheerful.

CHAPTER V

ONCE UPON A TIME
THERE WAS A CAT...

'...MADLY in love with a handsome prince. But though she cried and she mewed he didn't notice her. Finally, one day, her fairy godmother took pity on her and changed her into a beautiful girl with golden hair. The prince took one look at her and fell in love with her instantly and married her. But one night while the couple were happily sleeping, a rat appeared under the full moon, and crossed their chamber. The cat-girl saw it and, without thinking twice, pushed back the covers, leapt out of bed and pounced on it. The rat was caught, but alas, the princess's disguise was lost forever.'

Reworked and adapted for children, this story, originally written by Aesop over 2,500 years ago, is one of the delightful fables about cats.

Retelling it today is like taking a trip back to the days when books had lots of text and few illustrations, where fantasy wandered from adventure to adventure and we imagined everything our own size: magicians, castles, dragons and princes, with cats as heroines and heroes.

Inside the Magic Boots

Of all the figures of this enchanted anthropomorphic world, the most famous is undoubtedly Puss in Boots, created at the end of the seventeenth century by the highly regarded writer and member of the French Academy, Charles Perrault. Today no one remembers the names of his many learned volumes but everyone knows his *Contes de ma mère l'Oie*, a compendium of universally known fables like Cinderella, Little Red Riding Hood, Blue Beard, and Sleeping Beauty.

It is Puss in Boots though who stands out from the rest of his companions in the fables. What is striking is his mental clarity, the speed of his actions and how well he takes advantage of even the smallest occasion to achieve what he wants, which is to make his young and disinherited owner rich and obtain a royal marriage for him.

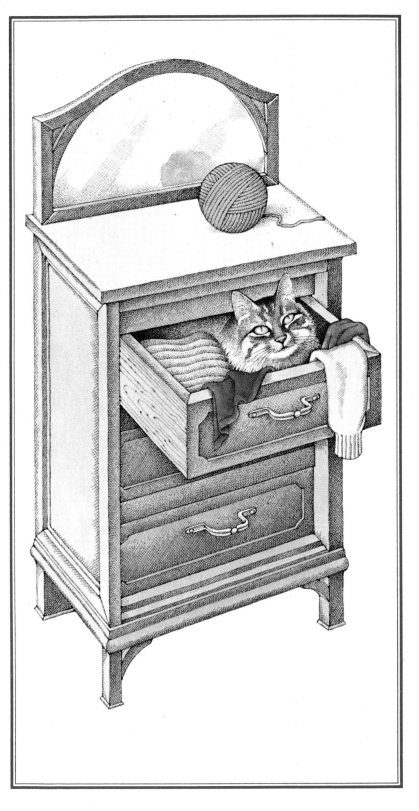

A precise marketing objective, we might say today, which our very able manager achieves with cold determination, a lack of preconceived ideas and a good dose of unavoidable cruelty.

Between tricks and deceptions, lies and clever schemes of all kinds, he reaches his goal and Perrault comments, 'Happy is the one who gets a rich inheritance from their family but even happier is the one who becomes rich and famous through their own talent and hard work.'

All of which in this case is thanks to the cat and its undeniable virtues, the same ones found in 'Dick Whittington and his Cat', one of the best-known cat stories in the English language.

A Coat of Arms

This time we are in London in the sixteenth century with ships sailing to the Orient laden with precious cargo to trade with rich sultans.

Dick Whittington is a poor lad alone in the world. His only inheritance is a small but handsome cat. Befriended by his employer, a rich merchant, Dick agrees to 'invest' his only riches, his cat, in a voyage in search of rich cargo his employer is sponsoring. During the voyage, the ship visits a country overrun with rodents. The cat is sold to the king to kill the rats and mice for ten times the worth of all the rest of the cargo. Thus, Dick Whittington's fortune is made, and the little cat's image becomes part of the Whittington family coat of arms forever after.

Dick Whittington was a real person who became Lord Mayor of London and there is even a monument erected to him which can still be seen in Highgate Hill. He and his cat's adventures were eventually transferred to the stage of the Drury Lane Theatre in London at the beginning of this century and they are still part of the traditional Christmas pantomime repertoire. Later, we shall see how much the cat likes the theatre and the spotlight.

Super Cat

For the moment, though, let us remain in London and take a look at the Victorian era when hypocrisy masked reality and the false front carried over into literature.

In this somewhat saccharine period, our friend was coaxed – without its consent and certainly without any pleasure in the role – into a false and ridiculous part, that of the impeccable and faithful children's tutor.

Gone is the wisdom and roguishness that had characterized it for centuries. Puss now became the protagonist of sentimental stories for the education and moral edification of young girls and boys.

Portraying silent composure, and a very clean, sweetly affectionate and lovingly maternal nature, little cats were also made the incarnation of the feminine domestic virtues expected of a good Victorian wife and mother.

And it is in this context and under this illusion that the absolute originality of Alice's fascinating cat comes through with its curious blend of magic and wise madness.

Alice's cat, from the illustration by John Tenniel

The Cheshire Cat

When the Reverend Charles Lutwidge Dodgson (better known as Lewis Carroll) published *Alice in Wonderland* in 1865, he could not have imagined that, of all the phantasmagorical animals created in stories throughout history, the most beloved and popular would be the Cheshire Cat.

A tabby cat with huge eyes and whiskers, looking rather like one of the cheeses from Cheshire (and thus its name), this incredible example of a cat – from the heights of a tree branch – behaves like a star, halfway between a vaudeville act and cabaret.

Using disappearing tricks, thanks to which it disappears and reappears at unexpected moments, or dissolves slowly into nothing, it unleashes a whole battery of observations in purest Anglo-Saxon nonsense style.

Thus, when Alice, distracted and confused, asks it 'would you tell me, please, which way I ought to go from here?' it answers, 'That depends a good deal on where you want to go'. 'I don't much care where . . .' replies Alice. 'Then it doesn't matter which way you go', concludes the cat with irrefutable logic. Later, in a fit of subtle wisdom, when it defines itself as mad in a land of lunatics, its proof is a pearl of laconic logic. 'A dog's not mad. You grant that?' 'I suppose so.' 'Well, then, you see a dog growls when it's angry, and wags its tail when it's pleased. Now I growl when I'm pleased and wag my tail when I'm angry. Therefore I'm mad.' 'I call it purring, not growling,' clarifies Alice. 'Call it what you like,' concedes our friend, magnanimously.

A cat like this was unique in the syrupy English writing of the era. This is confirmed by the fact that a few years later in *Through the Looking Glass* the same Carroll portrays Dinah and her three little ones as the most traditional domestic cats without the least touch of extravagant genius that one might have expected.

Was this a submission to the conventionalism of obtuse Victorian morality? So it would seem, given that the times were ripe – outside Albion at least – to demand extravagant cats with more anthropomorphic characteristics.

A Tuscan Cat on the Road

The first to create such a feline was an Italian. This was Collodi with his Pinocchio and the wretched cat that Pinocchio meets is the only one of its kind to end up in a fable as it really is.

Dirty, ragged and unfortunate, it is a poor vagabond getting along as best it can, far from the comforts of home, without protector, affection or a reliable source of food or shelter.

Life on the streets is rough, full of problems, unpleasantness and bad company. Its companion, the Fox, its *alter ego*, is a limping, untidy support.

Together the two get along as best they can, joining up with simpletons like Pinocchio so they can fill their bellies at least for a day. Altogether they are in only one chapter in the book, but they create a famous twosome and a way of speaking that has passed into current usage to describe two shady characters forever joined in their fraudulent and sly activities.

At heart, the Cat and the Fox are two poor devils burdened by Collodi's pen with all manner of physical

The Cat and the Fox from *Pinocchio* in the famous drawing by Chiostri

and moral ugliness so there can be no doubt about their function in the story, that of corrupting and leading astray scatterbrained youngsters with little judgement.

Poor cat! The one time a fable paints it as poor, ugly, alone, ill and unfortunate, it is also portrayed as vile, hypocritical, a liar and a traitor, giving fuel to the hateful fires of its detractors.

The Nemesis who Miaowed

Another poor cat, black and a bastard, but this time a faithful and unexpected instrument of Nemesis, had already given its name a few years earlier to a small literary work of art from the other side of the Atlantic. This was 'The Black Cat' by Edgar Allan Poe, a story (unsuitable for young audiences) of a drunk and his exaggerated hatred of the cat of the house. When the man, full of wrath, tries to murder it with an axe, his wife tries to defend it and in the ensuing fight he kills her.

He walls up her body in the basement and waits unafraid for the police. When they arrive, in a gesture of insolence and challenge, he swaggers around the rooms, hitting the walls with his cane. Suddenly there is a weak, but definite miaowing in response. He has inadvertently walled up the cat, alive, next to the corpse of his wife.

It reads like the chilling ending of a Hitchcock film in which implacable destiny and divine vengeance arrive right on time in the form of the cat.

The Diversion of a Nobel Prize

From the horrific images of Poe we move on to the fresh almost idyllic atmosphere of a time long ago, delightfully recreated by Kipling in one of his *Just So Stories* (1902).

This time the writer is not the poet of imperialism nor the flashy patriot nor the fascinating speaker with the voice of the jungle. 'The Cat that Walked by Himself' shows us instead the vigorous accomplished gift as fabulist of one of the great people of literature. The story that takes place long ago in prehistoric times, tells how and why the cat became domesticated.

In that hostile world where brute force was the only means of survival and where pacts and compromise and round tables were still to come, the unexpected happened, a civilized, democratic and composed agreement was made between a woman and a cat. She guaranteed it milk, a place by the fire and the leftover bones. Naturally, the cat also had its part in the contract. It would kill the mice and be kind to the babies so long as they did not pull its tail too hard.

This is how Rudyard Kipling saw the protagonist of his story, 'The Cat that Walked by Himself'

A Return to Childhood

Other favourites with whiskers and claws filled the stories of my childhood.

Patripatan for example, 'the most virtuous of all cats, the only one who went to heaven'.

So my grandmother, a very pious and religious woman, said when she told me of the adventures of that angora cat, honest through and through, a genuine benefactor of humanity, one of God's chosen.

I did not discover until a few years ago that this fable is an ancient Indian legend, with certain juicy details conveniently changed. The chaste Patripatan in reality possessed a harem with 365 lady cats, attended the erotic games at the court of Salangham and was more capricious, vain and unbearable than any other and was constantly asking the gods for expensive gifts.

'Spiegel Does Business' was, on the other hand, my father's favourite story. It came from the German with a precise date and author, 1850, Gottfried Keller, a Swiss writer.

In spite of its Germanic references, though, I must confess that at the time no other story pleased me more and I still feel a certain affection for it.

In brief, the story runs as follows: the cat Spiegel (which means mirror, so named because of its smooth, shiny fur) is forced to go hungry when its old mistress dies. Thin and parched, it makes a mephistophelean pact with the magician Pineiss: in exchange for food for three months, Spiegel will give up its own fat as a precious ingredient in the magician's witchcraft.

At this point, the story becomes a succulent and meticulous catalogue of all the sumptuous dishes it is given to eat: hot juicy sausages, oozing with fat, steaming in hundreds of huge pots, or grilled to a golden brown till they burst or roasted in the magician's fireplace . . .

My father at this point would fall into a dreamy reverie, remembering the beer halls and *heuriger* of Vienna, forgetting all about me and Spiegel and the end of the story, which of course was a paeon to the astuteness of the cat.

Because Spiegel, to save skin and fat, reveals to its jailor when the three months are up a fabulous hidden treasure: 300,000 ducats of gold, the dowry that a beautiful blonde maiden holds for the prince of her dreams who turns out to be Pineiss himself(!). But once the infamous contract between Spiegel and Pineiss is broken, it also breaks the spell of the Boticellian beauty, who in the bridal bed turns out to be a horrible obscene old witch, and just the wife for the cruel but clever magician.

And so it was that Spiegel went free and with a full stomach and so it is today that in Austria when someone thinks they have pulled off a good deal but in fact have ended up deceiving themselves, people say, 'Poor thing. They think they have bought the cat's fat'.

Girl with cat, an oleograph from Victorian times.

CHAPTER VI
THE COMIC STRIP THAT MIAOWED

IN the old days, when an animal spoke in a story, its words were enclosed in quotation marks like any other character. But if a drawing was made of it, it was portrayed as mute, quiet, as if surprised in the act. Animals were forced to lead double lives: a talking one in the narrative, and a silent one in the illustrations (when there were any!).

This division over the centuries became a kind of sickness draining force and vitality of expression from the cat's personality and multi-faceted ingenuity.

In the twentieth century however the two sides – illustration and dialogue – met, and the cartoon strip was created. And the first animal to snap out of its imposed lethargy and come to life as a character (and who continues to shine in the history of the comic strip) was the cat.

Krazy Kat, the Power of Love

George Herrimann, the cartoonist, forms part of the legend. A story is told about him that says when he was young and working as an apprentice baker, one day as a joke, he put a dead rat into a piece of dough and it was this act, together with his dismissal, that sealed his fate forever.

Searching for a new career, he decided to use his sense of humour and artistic talent and came up with the characters Krazy Kat and his arch-enemy, Ignatz Mouse. This time it was no practical joke, but on the contrary, a stroke of luck and he exploited it to the full.

For thirty-five years, against the squalid background of Coconino, Arizona, to the great delight of millions of readers and the despair of one poor mouse, he continued to invent the most surreal dialogues of incommunication imaginable. Krazy Kat, an androgynous cat, loved with a crazy passion the cursed Ignatz Mouse, who

I WAS CLEOPATRA ONCE SHE SAID.

Krazy Kat, George Harrimann's unforgettable creation

delighted in humiliating and chasing him, systematically dropping bricks on his head.

In spite of the nasty tricks played on him by the mouse and the incompetence of the obtuse and lazy police dog Officer Pupp, Krazy does not elude his stubborn pursuer but on the contrary is happy suffering what he considers displays of affection.

Like Isolde under the enervating effect of a magic potion, Krazy Kat lives, with innocent candour, in a world of dreams and quarrels and, though always ending up the loser, never suffers absolute defeat: the hate and indifference that surround him are pitted against the power of his immense love, moving it to a higher level of existence.

Felix the Cat: the Burden of Optimism

Inspired by the success of Krazy Kat, Herrimann invented another delightful comic-strip character in the twenties and gave it the exotic name of Mehitabel. An Egyptian cat, who sailed lazily down the Nile eating flowers and going back in her mind to a previous incarnation (in the guise of Cleopatra, no less!) she proved far too lazy – for public taste – to stop a new powerful force, that of superdynamo Felix the Cat. Created for the screen in 1917 by the Australian cartoonist Pat Sullivan, Felix made his début in the comics in 1923 and immediately won the sympathy of the whole world.

Candid and at times disconcerting, sometimes wise, sometimes foolish, but always a happy and faithful friend, Felix believed that in a crazy surreal world anything was possible: an exclamation point could be changed into a canoe, two question marks could become a pair of ice skates, two clouds and a branch could become a bicycle and a crescent moon a rocking chair.

There were no limits to his fantasy and his capacity to use every moment to his advantage. Precisely for that reason, Felix the Cat, champion optimist, dynamic and self-confident, reached the heights of popularity in the Depression years, becoming a model of inspiration for Americans.

Felix the Cat

In 1930, he became the first animated cartoon with sound and in 1932 he was chosen by Lindbergh to be his mascot on his famous transatlantic flight.

But in spite of all that, hard times lay ahead for our friend, at least on paper.

Peg Leg Pete: the Danger of Diversity

In 1928, after years of research and short clips, the anthropomorphic animal world of Walt Disney was born, the beginning of an astonishing success.

The only cat in his cast of characters was fat, ugly, stupid Peg Leg Pete. In the mind of Hollywood's Aesop, he was a vulgar, faithless criminal, an impostor and a liar, with such a bad temper that he was never able to keep cool long enough to defeat his mortal enemy Mickey Mouse. In spite of that, however, he managed to appear as a genuine, sincere character in a world populated by cheeky ducks, loopy dogs and lovable mice.

The early Peg Leg Pete was of a different fabric, but for fear that his differentness would alienate public sympathy, Disney changed him, making him more like the others.

He got rid of the stump and the ferocious gaze and

replaced them with a modern and efficient artificial leg and a charming smile and made him less aggressive – thus achieving his marketing objective. But it was a pity – Peg Leg Pete lost all his character, personality and charm. He became so sedate that he was even given a wife – fat, complacent Trudy – and his integration into the group was complete.

Tom and Jerry: Where Sadism Pays

The eternal struggle between cats and mice was to continue in the comics, but here – as a kind of vengeance and against nature – the latter were to defeat the former.

This was already true in the case of Krazy Kat and Peg Leg Pete but the greatest defeat of a cat was invented in 1939 by the remarkable team Hanna & Barbera, with Tom and Jerry.

Tom, the classic rat killer, is the kind of cat that in another era would have won praise, if only for the constancy with which he tries to catch that wily mouse, Jerry.

What happens in these episodes is worthy of an advanced course in sadism by the Marquis himself. Through page after page we follow almost identical but inexhaustible adventures full of all kinds of violence and torture, all taking place behind the doors of a peaceful American house.

Tom and Jerry in their eternal feud

The same thing happens with another cartoon cat, Sylvester, the frustrated assassin of his eternal enemy Tweety, a petulant canary with the razor-sharp mind of an eagle.

Fritz the Hippie Cat

In the mid-seventies, the cat made a comeback and it was dreadful. The standard bearer was one Fritz the Cat and in a single story he managed to break all the rules of legality and civilized behaviour. Oversexed and libidinous, a rebel, cynical and amoral, he smoked marijuana and organized orgies, becoming a symbol of an alienated youth 'hooked on videos' and the single-minded pursuit of sex.

The protagonist of an 'adults only' film which exalted his lascivious adventures (and smacked of both racism and a disturbing intolerance), Fritz enjoyed a brief life. More than different, he was just plain disagreeable, an uncomfortable mirror of a reality which everyone preferred to ignore.

The same quick death – again because of his meanness and cruelty – claimed another character, Fat Freddy's cat, one of the three Freak Brothers, who were a brief and surprising takeoff of the Marx Brothers.

The Aristocats, Cats as Cash-dispensers

In the same decade, Disney, who always bet – and rightly so – on long-term winners, held a finger to the wind and decided that cats would come back into fashion, but they would have to be sweet, ironic, amusing and charming loafers.

From this came 'The Aristocats', and soon the whole world was invaded by posters, dolls, pillows, glasses and a whole list of products inspired by the adventures of Duchess and her three kittens, Tu-Tu, Marie and Berly and their protector Tom O'Malley the alley cat.

It was the first large-scale commercial operation to take advantage of the growing cat mania. As always, the brains behind Walt Disney Productions were as clever as foxes. And yet, at the end of the seventies, there were new names looming on the horizon, with the same capacity for fantasy and money making.

Garfield: a Treasure

The first of these, Jim Davis, was a young man from Indiana who became famous and a millionaire after he created the irritatingly provocative face of Garfield.

Tiger-striped, with bulging Bette Davis eyes, fat and with a bewhiskered smile proclaiming his comfortable status as house cat, Garfield had not a drop of Krazy Kat's surreal lyricism or Felix's poetic charm. While not going as far as Fritz in his corruption, Garfield is impudent, outrageous, and loud but irresistibly roguish and terribly endearing.

'Cats are invincible', 'I'm fat and lazy and proud of it', 'A cat doesn't ask, it takes' (this in reference to a dish of lasagne left unguarded on the counter), are a few of his favourite mottoes, that he puts into practice not with the subtle weapon of purring but with the feisty punch of the boxer.

Garfield comes out every day in 1,150 American newspapers and for the last several years has filled, wallpapered and invaded the homes of millions of Americans with an infinite series of products in his image.

In royalties for this arrogant cat celebrity (including

That captivating cat, Garfield.

[56]

rights for use in advertising) Davis pocketed the tidy sum of $17 million in 1982. And to think there are still people who say cats are not useful!

A similar tale is the case of Bernard Kliban. His first book, a series of ironic vignettes about three house cats originally drawn to amuse his children and grandchildren, has been published in twenty-six editions and has sold more than a million copies. Kliban today is the head of a multinational industry set up to exploit his drawings on a wide range of objects from T-shirts to notebooks, pillows, bags and even – like Garfield – wallpaper.

A Dead Cat or A Dead Man?

The cleverest businessman of all however is Simon Bond who has made a fortune simply by venting his hatred (real or feigned) of cats.

In *A Hundred and One Uses of a Dead Cat*, Bond explores all the possible ways of using a dead cat (nicely embalmed of course). And he does it with such comic deception, such a surreal spark, far from any real sadism, that once one gets over the initial shock, one ends up bursting with laughter at his jokes.

There is an endless parade of cats – used as toasters, as tennis rackets, as vases, as arrows hitting a bull's eye, as umbrellas.

This macabre though innocuous sense of humour has not always pleased the millions of American cat-lovers and for them, Philip Lief has written and illustrated *Revenge of the cat: A Hundred and One Uses of a Dead Man*. The title says it all and its success forces us to think that finally the cat has reached the point of 'untouchableness' and perhaps it will not be long before the circle is complete – are we far from again proclaiming them gods Egyptian-style?

CHAPTER VII

MAD ABOUT CATS

> When I play with my cat, who knows whether she isn't amusing herself with me more than I am with her?
>
> *Montaigne (1533–1592)*

A Star-spangled Boom

THE fact that the cat is at the centre of a whole world of business in constant growth will come as no surprise to anyone. But in the United States it has reached what *Time* magazine has defined as an authentic national mania.

The subject of comic strips, books and toys, the image of the cat has now invaded the everyday life of American adults. It presides over calendars, blossoms on T-shirts, winks an eye on stamps, gives its name to cocktails, shines in logos, and figures on bags, beach umbrellas and all kinds of household goods.

The Metropolitan Museum of Art in New York opened a new room filled with canvases, sculpture and tapestries whose subject is the magnificent *Felis catus*. And the biggest Broadway success in years, 'Cats' by Andrew Lloyd-Webber, based on a book of poems by T S Eliot, *Old Possum's Book of Practical Cats*, has been hailed by critics and public alike for its original set and talented dancers, all of whom are made up as cats.

In the world of publishing, top American editors say that for a book to reach bestsellerdom, it needs four major ingredients: lots of sex, lots of intrigue, a bit of psychoanalysis and lots of cats.

Even in advertising, statistics show that a cat sells a product better than other images on television because it helps to fix the product better in our memory.

Shining Statistics

Certainly, cats are good business and they are everywhere (especially in the United States).

To be more precise, cats outnumber dogs in the US by 58 to 49 million. If one takes into account that in the last ten years this figure has been increasing at an annual rate of 55 per cent, it is time to say to the dog world, watch out, we have arrived.

One can only imagine the play of interest that this multitude of felines engages, exploiting the most varied feelings of passion, pride and guilt in their owners.

In terms of food, especially: French pâtés, Norwegian herring, delicious titbits of all kinds.

The annual investment in cat food, sold on television by real cat stars, reaches US$1.4 billion.

The most famous cat star is certainly Morris the Cat (actually Morris II), the Burt Reynolds of stardom, the macho cat who simply by eating a big helping of 9-Lives has charmed huge numbers of enthusiastic admirers on the other side of the small screen, and sent them off to buy his products. Morris, whose sophisticated voice is dubbed by the actor John Irwin, works about twenty days a year and earns a good $10,000 tax free.

The Life of an American Cat

Apart from being petted on demand, the happiness of a cat mainly depends on good food and a bowl of water, and where necessary a strategically placed litter tray.

But in fact the happiness of an American cat would seem to demand hundreds of extravagant accessories. Or at least so say a number of very serious cat psychologists, as they take advantage of a growing business in cats. And so apparently say many catophiles.

To give you an idea, there now exists a gadget for the cat spending the weekend alone. At predetermined times this gadget releases food (the most economical model is self-service: the cat can release food with his paw). For sleepy cats, there is a water bed called Cat-a-Lac. For cats dealing with stress, there is a rocking-horse-shaped bed; for the more independent ones, there is a catflap that is opened by a mechanism on the cat's collar, like an automatic electric garage door. If kitty feels nostalgic for the wild, there is a rug on which to sharpen its claws called Kitty Playground; for VIP cats you can have a Louis Vuitton cat carrier for the modest sum of $420 and for the thirsty pet, coca-cola brings you coca for cats!

California Dreaming

There is more. In California, bell-weather for the rest of the United States and the world, there is a chain of services that caters to every kitty need: big department stores, rest homes, rent-a-cat agencies, matchmakers, three cemeteries, two surgical clinics, a vacation spot, plus hotels offering all the amenities. Regarding the latter, Illinois takes the cake. In Prairie View, a cat motel offers private rooms, apartments and even prestigious presidential suites. Every afternoon at these luxurious residences, letters from their beloved owners off on holiday are read aloud to the kitty guests.

But let's go back to California, land of dreams and illusions for the cat and a gold mine for any businessperson with imagination.

Here, any kind of extravagance has a chance for success: singing competitions for the most musical miaow, Swedish massage and experts in cat muscles and backs, and most of all able psychoanalysts, expert in the mysteries of the cat psyche.

A good example is Ginger Hamilton, a fascinating doctor who created a whole new speciality and is now known as 'the feline Freud'.

Her speciality is emotional conflicts between cats and the new children or new companions of their owners. The problem is usually a matter of jealousy, pure and simple, but it can shatter domestic tranquillity with aggressive and vindictive behaviour by the cat who feels overlooked or replaced in its owner's affections.

It's no joke and can provoke a war of nerves, ripped curtains, shredded furniture, overturned tables and a number of denuded plants when a newborn baby or a new friend or lover upsets the familiar family atmosphere. Once mysteries such as leafless plants (used as amusing toys) have been solved, the problem of living together under new circumstances must be solved.

Anyone who has ever lived through this kind of situation can testify that only time can resolve certain things (like upholstery disasters) and others have no solution. Metro-Goldwyn-Mayer-style roars, fur standing on end, tails switching, unexpected swipes with razor-sharp claws, can last for years as 'symptoms' of the state of mind of a cat when presented with a hated intruder or a tiny new baby.

Only if the situation is faced with a certain amount of tolerance and unlimited patience and good humour can domestic peace ever be re-established. But there are limits. Not everyone can aspire to the level of diplomacy of one journalist who manages to keep happy four cats, two dogs, a toucan, a very tiresome mina bird, a crow, two children constantly surrounded by a crowd of friends, and last but not least, a very neurotic live-in lover.

A more typical situation occurs when the cat of the house has already decided how many people should live there and then new and disturbing factors (like children or new spouses) are introduced, and everything is turned upside down.

The one who will lose out – naturally – will not be the new baby. More likely, it will be the old cat.

This is probably also true of the new friend, although ultimately it depends on who takes up more space in the heart of the owner of the house, and a fat and adorable cat does require a lot.

Cats and Psychoanalysis

Let us return though to Dr Hamilton who has taken a different and very American stance: psychoanalysis for all!

Her therapy consists of speaking first individually to everyone involved: children, adults and cats. Then a group session is used to explore the past by delving into the subconscious, lingering especially (but how?) on the early post-natal experiences of the cat when mother cat was teaching her babies to keep clean and eat their food.

This seems to be the key which determines the future pyscho-affective evolution of the cat as well as future jealousies and what they imply.

It remains a mystery how Dr Hamilton manages to extract all this from the purrs and miaows and probably outbursts of temper from the poor cat, closed up in an unknown office with the very children, women and men that it hates most.

What is known is that this female Freud had quadrupled her income in only two years and that her appointment book is full for the next eighteen months. Compared to her, poor Cagliostro was an amateur.

And in Britain?

There are 6.5 million cats in 4.4 million households in the United Kingdom, not to mention large numbers of street cats, alley cats and strays. And of the 4.4 million households with a cat, 31 per cent have more than one. These pampered pets lead lives of privilege as good as any in the United States.

British cats annually consume some 4,795,000 tonnes of cat food, nearly 95 million hundredweight, a figure that increases by about 4.6 per cent each year and, for the insatiable appetite of these bewhiskered beasts, this means tins and dried food and gourmet cat pâtés enriched with plenty of vitamins.

As for creature comforts and vices, the British do not quite reach the heights of the Americans but in pet shops and department stores, all kinds of toys and gadgets for the amusement and pleasure of the most spoiled cat can be found: little cloth mice filled with catnip, small plastic balls with bells inside, scratching posts, nail clippers,

brushes and combs, shampoos, you name it, it can be found.

Useful Addresses

As for specialized stores in Britain and the United States, there are hundreds. In London, the large department stores, especially Harrods and John Lewis, have good pet supply departments. In the United States, most large cities have specialized pet stores and a glance at the local directories will give you some addresses.

If you want a cat of your own, the animal rescue leagues in Britain have a constant supply. A good place to start if you just want a 'moggy' would be to contact a local branch of The Cats Protection League (17 Kings Road, Horsham, West Sussex RH13 5PP) or to look in your local paper. Often your local vet will know about new litters.

For a pedigree, you can write for a list of breeders to the Governing Council of the Cat Fancy in Britain, 4–6 Penel Orlieu, Bridgwater, Somerset TA6 3PG, or the Cat Fanciers' Association, 9509 Montgomery Road, Cincinnati, Ohio 45242, the largest of many cat organizations in the US.

Finally, one last address that every good cat fancier should have and visit at least once: the Cat Museum in Riehen, Switzerland, near Basilea, Baslerstrasse 101.

CHAPTER VIII

CATS AND CELEBRITIES

Cruel, but composed and bland,
Dumb, inscrutable and grand,
So Tiberius might have sat,
Had Tiberius been a cat.

Matthew Arnold (1822–1888),
'Poor Matthias'

Powerful Owners

NO one knows the name of Cleopatra's cat but the famous queen was inspired by its eyes to paint an exaggerated line around her own with black kohl. Mohammed doted on his Muezza and he must surely have spoiled it since, rather than wake it, he preferred to cut off the part of his garment the cat was sleeping on. Richelieu left his fourteen cats an inheritance of one of the apartments in his sumptuous residence in Paris. Powerful Cardinal Wolsey (at the court of Henry VIII) could not bear to be separated from his huge tabby even when he was saying mass at Westminster. The Earl of Southampton celebrated his release from the Tower of London in 1603 by having his portrait painted with Trixie, his faithful cat companion in prison. Among the famous English politicians and cat-lovers were Anthony Eden, Harold Wilson and Winston Churchill, who allowed himself to be photographed in his office along with his three cats.

The funny thing is that in every century, in every country, a long list of the famous have risked the ridicule of the uncomprehending and chosen a cat as their ideal companion.

A dog can watch your property, hunt and offer protection. The cat simply fascinates. Its aesthetic gracefulness, its velvety silence and the mystery behind its magic eyes have always bewitched painters and artists who have immortalized it in endless works, making it co-protagonist (for example in Manet's famous portrait 'Olympia') and even protagonist (think of Ligabue's splendid lion cat). But more than painters, it has been poets and writers who have been most fascinated by cats.

Canis Hominis Amicus, Felis Poetae

For Petrarch, his beloved cat, as he himself confessed, came second only to his Laura. For Tasso, 'Lights in my study, oh beloved cats', were his companions in his darkest years.

Samuel Johnson fed his Hodge with oysters from Brittany; Victor Hugo built his adored Gavroche a kind of throne as a bed; Chateaubriand, who idolized cats, received as a gift, or rather an inheritance, the cat of Pope Leo XII, which stayed with him to his death; George Sand shared her morning milk with Minou, drinking from the same cup; Dumas Fils declared himself, in the Hermitage of Montecristo, 'defence lawyer' for all the stray cats that he found and protected – the same ones (if a bit fatter) that Baudelaire called 'friends of science and pleasure', and Anatole France called 'silent guardians of my city of books'.

Theophile Gautier, justifying his love for cats, said: 'Pashas love tigers and I love cats because cats are the tigers of us poor devils.'

Beloved, adored and immortalized in poetry and prose, the tutors and muses of women and men of letters, cats have always enjoyed a special immunity and exclusive privileges. They are the only ones allowed to penetrate the inner sanctum of the study, walk through the library, pass among the pens and inkwells and sit right in the middle of the latest page of the masterpiece or make a mess of the pile of notes and drafts of future masterpieces.

So far I have been speaking of the past but the same can be said about the present, for cats have always loved the silence of libraries, the smell of books and the rustle of turning pages. Nonchalantly, they bat erasers about, chew the corners of book covers and, in the twentieth century, play a new game of walking over the typewriter keys.

A writer's dog stays at the feet of the owner, in the servile and yearning hope that she or he will finish their work and take it out for its daily walk, while the cat jumps on its owner's table among all the work papers with the arrogance of a lord who does not ask for anything, giving off a mysterious psychic energy.

A magic potion of communication runs between them . . . And the pen flies faster.

Many great writers have known (and taken advantage of) this happy union, from Rousseau to Sartre, from Sir Walter Scott to Mark Twain, fron Byron to Henry James, from Anatole France to Cocteau, from Colette to Jorge Luis Borges, from Dickens to Buzzati.

Aldous Huxley once said, 'If you want to write, keep cats'. But apparently one was not always enough. When Hemingway was writing *A Farewell to Arms* he had thirty-four bewiskered friends running around his house in Cuba – though it was quite a big house.

Edward Lear had a big striped cat named Foss whom he immortalized in his drawings although the real Foss had a very short thick tail. Dickens too was very fond of cats and they featured in several of his books, notably the elderly cat belonging to Mrs Pipchin in *Dombey and Son* and the various cats in *Bleak House*. Dickens himself had a favourite white cat named William (who later became Williamina after it produced a litter of kittens).

Henry James and Raymond Chandler were two more who kept these sources of inspiration. And surely one must include Hamlet, the cat who lived at the New York hotel, the Algonquin, a favourite haunt of literati for years.

The Cat Accused

Last but not least, we have the case, as the authors of the classic mystery or detective novel would say, of Enzo Ferrea, a writer of English-style mysteries. At the heart of his plot there is always an assistant to Detective Camillo, also known as Gaylord von Semarang, a kind of Doctor Watson in a long snow-white coat with greyish-blue paws and muzzle, and enormous round eyes which give him a noble and mysterious appearance. The cat, a noble bluepoint Persian who, armed only with his sense of smell, his claws and his wit, is an invaluable help in the brilliant resolutions of the most intricate cases, especially in 'When My Little Mama Died' which won the Tedeschi prize for best detective novel.

Certainly the cat today not only serves as a stimulus to creativity, it also adds a touch of grandness and worldliness to those it lives with or who show it off as a status symbol.

Superstar Cats

Other notable cat owners were Queen Victoria, who had a big white Persian named Heather, and Caroline and John Kennedy who had a little cat named Tom Kitten. Theodore Roosevelt's son Kermit also had a cat when his father was in the White House. He named it Tom Quartz after a character in one of Mark Twain's books, *Roughing It*.

Many of the cats of the famous were Persian and Persian implies worldly. Their expression of constant bad temper, their fluffy coats, compact and incredibly soft, their lazy yet noble walk and disdainful behaviour have made them the aristocrats of cats, a precious and wonderfully cared for work of art. Not surprisingly both Giorgio Armani and Franco Zeffirelli have Persians.

CHAPTER IX

THE CAT AS SEX SYMBOL

Cats Live for Sex

THIS is neither a proverb nor a popular saying. It is what people say who know cats well, especially when they live with them.

A male or female cat in heat seems to burn with desire, it cries out, it calls, it howls with a range of sounds and vibrations that not even a moog synthesizer could imitate. And while this is going on, the owner of this volcano of passion shouts and cries from lack of sleep or at the very least begs for peace and quiet. Nervous exhaustion is one step away and Hamlet's dilemma takes on a feline tone – suicide or caticide. Considering that an average female cat can become a mother three or four times a year and can come into heat every three weeks, especially in spring, and every birth produces three to five kittens – this is clearly no small problem.

An Operation for a Good Cause

For the city cat, the only solution is sterilization or castration. Many people are opposed to such drastic surgery and they make strong libertarian arguments against it, hinting at Nazism and worse. But let's look at the reality. During these spasmodic episodes of courtship, a cat needs to be free of domestic enclosures. The pursuit of a warm body becomes for our friend – who just days earlier had been a bit of a homebody – an experience of elucidation, privation, violence and fights to the death.

Some eventually come home but in a pitiful state (blind, ill-nourished, covered with scabs and fleas), others never come home at all. In any case, the average lifespan of a city cat turned vagabond is two years compared to twelve to fourteen years and even longer for a house cat.

Forget the idea that 'castrated cats become fat and stupid'. They become fat by eating too much and leading a sedentary life (probably resulting from a guilt complex on the part of their owners) and stupid is simply not possible: a stupid cat is a contradiction in terms.

If you mean to say they become dull (or worse) it is because they are not getting enough affection and a cat ignored can become truly sick with melancholy (but not stupid!).

Cats and Women

If a cat's sexuality is disconcerting and shocking, its sensuality, on the other hand, has always been bewitching because of its analogy to another much more disturbing and mysterious world for men, the world of women. It is a world men can conquer, violate, suffocate, study or love, but never completely understand. This feminine world is unfathomable in its infinite variety of intimate and hidden treasures, its reckless generosity, its lanquid abandon and unexpected passions, its feigned flights, ingenuous acts of cruelty and irresistible caprices, its raging jealousies and dark and stubborn spitefulness . . . how much of this cats and women share!

And how many poets and writers have recognized it, using (and abusing) the comparison in their writings.

> Come, my beautiful cat, to my loving heart,
> Pull in your claws,
> And let me fall into your beautiful eyes,
> Which gleam like metal and agate.

This was written by Baudelaire to his cat but would he have written anything very different if his lover were the obscure object of desire?

> As my fingers lazily caress
> Your head and supple back,
> And my hand grows drunk with pleasure
> Touching your electric body,
>
> I seem to see my wife. Her look,
> Like yours, lovable beast,
> Deep and cold, cuts and wounds
> Like a dart.

In these few lines, the analogy could not be more daring. Maupassant, the writer of the poem, does the same in another work when, buried deep in a soft couch, among the sounds of rustling taffeta and satin, with his accomplice, 'an enormous black cat that She adores', he seizes the opportunity and takes the woman's hand, letting his fantasies run free. 'Our fingers met on the animal's back and caressed each other under his silky fur. I felt against my cheeks the trembling rounded hip . . .' But whose hip? One imagines it is the cat's, since he goes on to speak of its paws and its melodious purring (unless of course his love had started purring!).

The French were not the only ones who highlighted this correspondence between the amorous and the feline. The Russians were not far behind: 'I kissed her head . . . and the little kitten came to life; her eyes shone and she seemed to get ready to switch her tail as is natural to them.' Natural only up to a point, since he is referring to a girl, Sonia, the cousin of Natasha Rostova, in love with Nicolas Rostov in *War and Peace*. Sonia is a fragile creature whom Tolstoy always compares to a tender little kitten because of her nervous and passionate emotions.

The Woman-Cat Par Excellence

Colette, candid, impudent, arrogant and maliciously tender, was a free spirit, yet one madly enslaved to love, a woman of provocative beauty, a fascinating actress and, above all, a writer with a very keen sensual imagination.

She was like a cat and she loved and understood them like no one else. In the midst of the frantic disorder of her emotional life, cats were always her best friends and the greatest inspiration for her masterpieces.

'Yes, there have been lots of dogs in my life [these are her words], but there has also been the cat. To the race of cats I owe a certain sense of dissimulation, of keeping a space around myself, with a special aversion to loud sounds, and a need to keep silent for long periods.'

Perhaps it was in the role of cat, in one of those profound osmoses that are the secret of the theatre, that Colette found a way to understand and reach an expressive synthesis of everything that had built up inside her and made her tick. Was it because she felt and lived her own sexuality so intensely? Was it this that, according to some people, made her identify with the disconcerting amorous fantasies of a cat in heat?

A Lethal Threesome

Cat, woman, pleasure. An explosive mixture potentially more dangerous than napalm. In every century, lovers have been burned by it, writers and painters inspired by it.

In the last century, advertising joined the ranks and exploited the provocative similarities, beginning at the end of the nineteenth century with women's lingerie. The players were brassières and girdles, filmy panties, lush beauties and, naturally, lanquid cats.

As it continued into our century, the women wore less and less and the cat grew more malicious and flattering among a profusion of brassières and silk stockings, high-heeled slippers with pompons and baby-doll pyjamas.

Today cats are still there selling furs and jewels, drinks and perfumes, and any other object that is meant to seduce, seduce, seduce.

The identification cat-woman continues, a perfect and happy fusion that fortunately is no longer punished by burning at the stake.

CHAPTER X

IDENTITY PARADE

A Quick X-Ray

FELIS *domesticus*: average length, 15–20in/40–50cm, plus 12–14in/30–5cm of tail. Shoulder height, about 12in/30cm. Weight, 8–10lb/4–5kg with 288 bones, 517 muscles, 51 vertebrae, 26 ribs, 30 teeth and 18 claws, 10 in the front feet and 8 in the back. Tongue covered with tiny abrasive papillae. Pear-shaped stomach, liver divided into five parts. Lateral whiskers that serve as a kind of radar. Two eyes, each with a visual field of 200 degrees. Pupils extremely dilatable because of a special light-conserving mechanism, the *tapetum lucidum*. Unmistakable purring noise, which can sound like a motorcycle, during moments of profound satisfaction of subject in question.

These characteristics are common to all cats. But there are many breeds, each with their own peculiarities. As it would take an encyclopaedia to catalogue them all, we will limit ourselves to a brief description of ten of them, as a general overview, so that next time you go to a cat show, you will know what to look for.

Shorthaired Cats
Abyssinian

The king of cats, a direct descendant of the Egyptian *mau*. Noble and proud, with thick, short hair that is a brindled brown or grey.

The Abyssinian Cat Club was founded in 1926 in their honour to protect their purity and educate the public. Recently the price of the breed has risen sky-high: one red Abyssinian sold for $3,000 in California.

American Shorthair

The first American shorthairs went over with early British settlers. A bit bigger and longer than the British shorthair, with a slightly more oval head, they come in all colours and patterns.

Used on the early settlers' ships as a rat killer, the

American shorthair is today a hardy and brave cat. The head is oval shaped with a square muzzle and large, round eyes that are slightly slanted at the corners.

British Shorthair

This cat has a strong, muscular body with short legs and a thick, short coat. It has a broad, rounded head and big, round eyes. There is a wide range of fur colours and patterns.

Most of the British shorthair breeds were developed in the nineteenth century but they all are descendants of the ordinary street cat. They are good-natured, intelligent and affectionate.

Burmese

These were sacred, and venerated like gods, in the monasteries of Mandalay. One was stolen in the middle of the nineteenth century by an American sailor and introduced into the United States. The breed has fine, glossy fur, a triangular-shaped head with a prominent chin and golden-yellow, almond-shaped eyes.

When a Burmese is born its fur is a light coffee-colour which grows darker until it is a deep rich brown by the age of one year. It is very vocal and, to judge by the attentive way it watches everything through the window of the car or train, it loves to travel.

Manx

This is the famous tail-less cat from the Isle of Man. The story goes that it arrived late for Noah's Ark and got its tail caught in the door. In reality, it seems that several were brought on board ships in Malaysia by sailors who were part of the Armada and they ended up shipwrecked near Ireland around 1589.

It is not only the lack of a tail that makes these cats interesting but also their hind legs, which are longer than their front legs, causing them to jump like a rabbit (which in fact they resemble a bit because of their short, soft fur, their short body and rounded rump).

Scottish Fold

This is called the fox-terrier of cats because of its curiously folded-over ears. Imported from China at the end of the nineteenth century (by the usual sailor, this time Scottish), it was bred mostly in Scotland. It has a round body, a wide head, round eyes and a long nose. There are several varieties of colouring.

In its native land, this cat was compared to a dog (the chow to be precise) for the delicate flavour of its meat. It was often served at the tables of the Mandarins as a delicacy.

Siamese

For some, Thailand, for others Indo-China in general, but in either case it came from the Far East. From the first two pairs who arrived in London in 1885 (called Pho and Mia, Tiam O'Schian and Suzan) the English breeders have developed six varieties based on the colour of their fur, ranging from browns to lilacs.

It is the perfect child of our times, ultra-sensitive, unpredictable, aggressive and with a strange sense of humour. Very intelligent, fastidious and a bit of a sex maniac, it is able to sacrifice its exuberance to a lead and is not above a little walk with its adored (and only) owner.

Longhaired Cats
Birman

Stolen by a faithless servant from the temple of the Dalai Lama and transported after a thousand detours to North America where a Vanderbilt paid for its weight in gold, the first Birman arrived in the United States in 1918. It has a long, cream-coloured coat with golden accents, a plume-like tail and magnificent violet-blue eyes à la Elizabeth Taylor.

Often referred to as a longhaired Siamese, it is different from all other cats because the front paws are gloved in white and the back paws are also partially white.

Colourpoint Longhair

This is an invented breed, developed in the thirties as a cross between a longhair and a Siamese. It gets is colouring and blue eyes from the Siamese and the full, long, thick coat, short, stocky body and snub nose from the longhair.

Colourpoint kittens are born white and they don't develop their unusual markings fully until they are eighteen months old. They have a characteristic sweet, musical voice.

Persian

It is said that an explorer, Pietro dalla Valle, imported several cats around 1550 from the Korassan region but others give all the credit to Turkey and an eighteenth-century archaeologist, Nicolas Fabri de Peinex. In any case, it was the English as usual who began to develop the breed scientifically. Although there are many differences in the colour and pattern of the fur, the common characteristics of this showy cat are a wide, round head, full cheeks, a short, upturned nose, round eyes, a short, cobby body and a full-plumed tail.

Occasionally a Persian will have two eyes of different colour and this fascinating defect disqualifies them from shows. The white Persian resembles an Angora, a rare cat which at one time was the favourite of the concubines of the pashas.

The New Breeds

Mutants sometimes result from crossbreeding and the following four appear only at the most elegant shows and are extremely expensive.

Ragdoll

A languid concoction of fur and muscles looking vaguely like a Birman.

Cornish Rex

A curly or wavy coated cat with enormous, triangular ears.

Turkish

A cousin of the Angora with a white coat and reddish-coloured tail and ears. It loves to swim.

Sphynx

A completely hairless breed. Smooth skinned, without hair or wrinkles or even whiskers, the poor thing is not a very attractive specimen.

CHAPTER XI
CAT HOROSCOPES

The Feline Zodiac

COLETTE once said, 'There are no normal cats'. 'And no two alike', I would add. Each cat has its own habits and weaknesses and moments of wild tenderness.

Cats are just as individual as we humans are. In fact, they are probably even more so.

Their capricious and multi-faceted personalities make them the ideal subject not only for psychoanalysis (as the United States can testify) but also for astrology, something we can all learn about.

Excluded from the tight mysterious link that binds a cat to the astral world and guides it with absolute autonomy, at least we have recourse to the stars for different and equally valid motives.

Knowing the horoscopic characteristics of the cat will allow us to understand its nature better – a homelover or a rover, shy or outgoing. It will also establish a solid base for a happy and harmonious life together (and in these times it is one of the few partnerships that gives genuine pleasure with little sacrifice).

If a cat is bought or is a present from friends, it is quite easy to find out its date of birth. But you may have brought home a stray or saved a cat from the hands of some cruel person, or one fine day there it was on your doorstep or in a corner of the garden or on the roof.

The poor thing will know immediately how to capture your heart (it comes with being a cat!) but will know nothing about its genealogy. The following notes, taken from astrological studies and long personal experience, may help. If you read them carefully, you can discover very quickly what sign your cat is.

If you find that some of its extravagances or other personality quirks that drive you mad are confirmed, remember no one is perfect and (as Lady Sidney Morgan once rightly said) 'a kitten is much more amusing than half the people one is obliged to live with'.

[77]

Aries (March 21–April 19)

Aggressive, indefatigable, the Aries cat seems to have been born to revolutionize things around it: life, customs, habits.

One night it will sleep quietly at your feet, the next it will take it into its head to climb to the top of the bookcase (with the ensuing crash of books and small objects) and another night it will quietly install itself behind a curtain to wait for dawn and the arrival of the first bird.

Its extravagances will drive you wild but its jealousy will charm you. It will come only to you and stick to you like glue, growling like a dog if you so much as speak to the canary (who in any case will have a brief and tormented life).

Taurus (April 20–May 20)

Spirited and plump, Taurus cats often have thick fur that gives them an unmistakable look of softness. They love to be picked up and when they are, they relax completely with dreamy eyes, drooping tail and exaggerated purring. And yet one always wonders if it is all just a comic act to divert your attention from some felony committed.

Peaceful and home loving, they have no particular demands but if they get an idea in their head, you can be sure they will persist until they achieve it.

Healthy, sweet and affectionate, they are the best company. But don't provoke them needlessly because they spit and scratch like no other.

Gemini (May 21–June 20)

Passionate, edgy, exuberant, the Gemini cat is made for sex and the adventurous life of the wide open spaces. It does not like schedules or punctuality. Don't ask it to sleep on the same cushion every day or to sit on your lap while you watch television.

Instead put on your Florence Nightingale outfit when it comes home beaten and unrecognizable after a late night session on the roofs or be prepared to stock up on warm little baskets and lots of tiny bottles because

Mother Gemini won't hang around long to take care of the little things. The free and easy life, full of the unexpected, is the one for effervescent Gemini.

Cancer (June 21–July 22)

You should not be offended if the moody and slightly mad Cancer showers you with affection one day and the next won't even look at you.

It has its ups and downs, it is true, but it will always remain close to you, never abandoning you for feline crusades. The classic sphynx of the hearth, it can't stand guests, especially noisy children. In fact all it really likes is you and the house.

Super sensitive, it does not like jokes at its own expense. As revenge it is quite capable of hiding in an old suitcase or box or under the bed or the cupboard or behind the refrigerator and leaving you searching for it for hours on end.

Leo (July 23–August 22)

Proud and vain, the Leo cat is very much aware that it is a direct descendant of some noble cat.

Even walking through dark streets and over steeply pitched roofs, its stride is proud.

It likes to be fussed over, brushed and petted from head to tail, which it will hold high like a glorious standard.

Cheerfully argumentative, it will always look for a way of getting attention to show off its superiority.

On nights of love, its cry – at times deep, at times sharp – will keep a whole neighbourhood awake. This will be repeated periodically.

Virgo (August 23–September 22)

Sweet, patient and a profound thinker, the Virgo is prudent by nature. Since it was little it knew just how far it could go and, as for flights up the curtain, it would prefer something less risky such as the hypnotic effect produced by watching the goldfish swim in the bowl.

A cat which easily feels the cold, it spends the winter curled up by the radiator and the summer chasing the sun. The other seasons are tragic for it but it faces them bravely.

If you really want to make a Virgo happy, leave the television on as much as possible for there is nothing it likes better then lying on top of the warm machine, though you must be sure to keep the volume turned right down.

Libra (September 23–October 22)

Sophisticated, elegant, with a certain aplomb, this is the classic show cat.

Luxury is its natural habitat, a 'golden calm' its preferred atmosphere. Let it stay in soft upholstered surroundings, especially antique ones. Don't scrimp on the satins and taffetas or the goosedown pillows. You will find that it is the ideal companion, never allowing itself to get muddy.

You must show it a lot of love, especially if it is a common alley cat or a mixed breed and not (as it would like to think) a pure-bred Persian. In such cases, be discreet and protect it from an inferiority complex. If there is nothing else you can do about it, at least name it Byron or Greta or Napoleon.

Scorpio (October 23–November 21)

Impetuous, exuberant, shocking, this is the cat athlete *par excellence*.

Instead of walking, it runs; it will break into a gallop with its tail held high, then just as suddenly stop, stupefied. It climbs the curtains, throws itself off the top of the door, leaps on to the cornices, rips out the geraniums, throws itself on your bed in the middle of the night.

A cyclone like this one will guarantee you a heart attack, arguments with the neighbours and high bills. But on the other hand, it will be beloved by upholsterers, clothes-repairers and glaziers, all of whom will be guaranteed regular work.

Sagittarius (November 22–December 21)

This cat does not want problems, it just wants to be left alone to get on with its life.

A lazy glutton with fixed habits, what it really likes is lots of peace and quiet and lots of food. It is a good host cat: it always knows how much food is on hand, it will preside over the preparation of the meal with great attention, it will count the number of bites you have taken and its favourite fantasy is that you will be called to the phone in the middle of a meal. It can compete with the best dishwasher – there is no equal to its tongue – and it can make the worst grease on a plate disappear.

Capricorn (December 22–January 19)

Put on your white gloves if you are going to live with a Capricorn. Treat it affectionately, be delicate, kind and completely gentle. The Capricorn cat is very reserved and modest and verges on being a snob.

Many cats of artists, poets and writers fall under this sign. They adore typewriter keys, the rustle of paper and the smell of books and they are rapturous if they see a picture of themselves in a fashion magazine.

You can make them happy by making them famous or at least letting them think they are. It won't be difficult because they are very gullible.

Aquarius (January 20–February 18)

Finicky or epicurean? It is hard to know. In either case, food for Aquarians is something to be taken very seriously.

Don't even think of giving it leftovers from your meal. It will not protest but it will despise you from the depths of its heart and go on a hunger strike.

Generally this little joke will be repeated once a week, if only to keep you on your toes over the quality and freshness of the fish you feed it, preferably sole or salmon and, please note, it prefers the first rare and the second grilled.

Pisces (February 19–March 20)

Flowers are a Piscean's passion. It doesn't matter if they are fresh, dried or potted. It will always believe that you have bought them just for its personal pleasure.

When it does not eat them petal by petal, it pulls them out of the vase and, Carmen-like, runs about the house with a flower in its mouth. My advice, if you wish to prevent big holes in the garden and broken vases inside, is to give up your green fingers and find another hobby.

'Woman with Cat' by Mario Sironi; a pencil drawing

CHAPTER XII
HAPPINESS IS A WARM CAT

A DOUBT suddenly enters my mind. I stop to think. Then I go back over what I have written. In this cocktail of a book, I have thrown in a little bit of everything: history and literature, anecdotes, statistics, proverbs and sayings, poetry and humour. The cat cocktail is served. But it still lacks something. The maraschino cherry? The sliver of pineapple? The mint leaf? Who knows?

Maybe it needs the fiery colour that certain Dutch liqueurs give? Or the strong flavour of rum, or the perfume of a drop of bitters? That enjoyable, soft, round warmth that is the very essence of cat and that perhaps I have not been able to transmit.

The truth is that I have conveyed the voices of history and poets and farmers and sailors and the voices of bigwigs of yesterday and today, even mummies and fanatics throughout history, but what I have forgotten is that of everyday life.

I have looked at it all through the wrong end of the telescope, from the outside, from the past or a distant present, explaining certain tales and adventures of the cat, but forgetting the most exciting part of all, daily life with 'him' (or in my case with 'her').

After travelling all over the map, here I am, back on my own doorstep, and there, dignified, attentive and serious sits Suzy, my prototype for universal 'catness'.

For four years we have lived in perfect symbiosis. At first she had pinkish eyes, three pitiful whiskers and a scrawny fringe of a tail. Over the years she has become quite a lady with lots of fur and eyes the colour of the weather, a sort of green-violet-yellow that makes me think of tropical sunsets after a hot rainstorm in August.

If I think of what she means to me and my life, I cannot help but feel lucky compared to others.

What 'others'? Well, the ones who do not have cats, of course. Poor specimens of human beings, among them two friends undergoing psychoanalysis, three in sensitivity training, my ex-husband and his Shiatzu and my sister-in-law with her guru.

I, on the other hand, have Suzy, my fifth gear, my anchor against stress, my port in the storm.

Better than a Tranquillizer

There is a bestseller in France (with the revealing title *Le Psy-Chat*) in which the author, Odette Eylat, maintains that 'the cat, loved, sought out or repulsed, like the psychiatrist, reconstructs for us the severed umbilical cord with Mother Nature, with the infinite'.

The ancients knew this as the arcane hypnotic power of the cat and today it still is a secret 'remoter than the Ganges and the sunset', in Borges's words.

I, too, when I want to absent myself, relax, let my thoughts wander and feel like an octopus carried by the waves, instinctively look for Suzy, the perfect mirror of my life. I want to absorb her round seraphic personality, decipher her dreams lost in time, live my days the way she does, without tumult or embarrassment, busy only with relaxing pleasures.

A Real Talent for Comfort

Curled up in an egg-shape next to the radiator, nestled in a pillow or sprawled lazily in the bathtub, Suzy knows everything about the pleasures of relaxation and comfort according to season.

In winter, she can find, with a single glance, my cashmere cardigan to sleep on, the hidden pipe that heats the room or the television, warm from being left on for hours, and down she plops, tail hanging.

In summer she soon discovers the coolness of the marble tabletop, or the way in which the breeze and the shade under the wisteria give a shiver of light, vibrant freshness. In any season she adores rustling papers, corners, high places and the half-open drawers of the chest where she can knead a little nest.

I always leave her happily in peace, I have never tried to domesticate (!) her or impose on her, because of some whim or desire of my own, some illogical restriction. I respect her sacred dreams, provide her with a varied diet, give her catnip and a clean dish, only pet her as much

as she wants to be petted, and sometimes tease her with slightly mischievous toys like a chicken leg or a couple of feathers or a little stuffed animal in the shape of a mouse.

'Even the smallest feline is a work of art'

So thought the genius Leonardo da Vinci but still there are people who like cats and people who don't.

People, for example, who confuse a cat's reserve with indifference, their spirit of independence with betrayal, their natural instinct for hunting with cruelty, or their innate dignity with selfishness. People who have invented pejorative expressions like catty, cat burglar, catcall and cat's paw.

Even though they may pretend to like cats, people like this are quickly exposed. It makes it even worse if they try to win over a cat by treating it like a dog (with pats on the head, noisy flattery, and vigorous slaps on the back).

Cat protocol is even more strict than diplomatic protocol. It is based on individual and mutual respect, much like the Spanish or Latin American concept of 'honour'.

Some Advice

If you want to be friends with a cat, the best thing to do is nothing. Just look at it quietly, crouch down and wait until it comes to you. Let it sniff you if it wants to. Suzy generally prefers people's noses and here is where the secret cat-hater is unmasked because they think they are going to be scratched.

At this point, your cards have been played. If the cat stays near you, you can go one step farther and pick it up. But please, not by the scruff of its neck. Even though some veterinarians and so-called experts advise it, I think it is most undignified. Pick it up gently, under its belly, and support it with your left arm so it can rest its paws over your right hand.

You will feel at this point under the furry mass a bundle of nervous tension. There is a moment of suspense while the cat decides whether there is the possibility of a meaningful relationship with you.

If it decides in your favour, it will relax and get more comfortable, even (but this is almost reaching the level of the miraculous) begin to purr. This is your gold medal for having won over the sympathy of the creature.

On the other hand, if it stays tensed and you can see it is ready to jump down, let it go. If you restrain it you will end up with bad memories and will have lost the friendship of that cat forever.

I don't mean to suggest that if it does not accept you as something to sit on, it will not accept you as a person.

You may have been introduced to one who does not like being held (a frequent phenomenon). Letting it go free will give you points for tact and sensitivity in the cat's mind.

If you always remember that respect is the only fertile ground to plant in, you will cultivate a splendid friendship with a cat.

The Right Kind of Attention

More advice: never pull its leg. Never try to have fun at its expense. Cats are very proud and have absolutely no sense of humour.

It sometimes happens, for example, that Suzy miscalculates a jump or mistakes a black spot for a fly or attacks a butterfly and fails or sneezes when she smells pepper. If I laugh, it's all over. She will sulk for hours, her pride wounded. On the other hand, I can laugh with pleasure

at her silly threats, an art she has perfected over the years.

Let me explain.

Suzy has made it clear – at least if I want to get any sleep or work done – that she should always be the centre of my attention. So if I am occupied in the kitchen or reading or writing, or best of all, talking on the phone, she goes into action.

Within view, she hunts out her target object – which must be expensive or fragile or something I really treasure. It might be an engraved lighter, a little bottle of perfume, the grandfather clock or the remote control for the television. Tired of being ignored, but with a tactical patience, she waits until our eyes meet and then she points out with her right paw the object she has in mind. When I shout 'Suzy, no!' she stops for a moment and then with complete calm and innocence, she walks off.

'I wouldn't have done anything, you know,' she seems to say, while she ostentatiously begins to wash the paw in question and narrows her eyes maliciously.

Another typical show takes place in the morning.

If I am still not up at seven, her stomach alarm clock begins to ring and sets off a whole chain of events. She systematically, one after the other, decides to throw down five or six objects in noisy progression, from the smallest one farthest away to the heaviest one close to my bed. Firstly, it's my lipstick and makeup brush, then it is a framed photograph and my diary,and finally, my glasses and the music box next to my bed. This dance of the seven veils becomes my daily wake-up call, with no need for an alarm clock.

I ended up carpeting my bedroom for this very reason – that music box was the best one in my collection.

'Marry for merriment and boredom will not come between you'

Cats are truly funny and enormously cheerful. It is funny when Suzy opens closed doors (although it is true anguish for her) jumping on the handle with her paws together; it is funny to watch her run, tail held high when she sees some food in her dish; it is funny when she walks in with a carnation between her teeth that she has just pulled out of a vase; it is funny when she glares at me as I ease into a hot bath (because it is one of her favourite places when empty); funny when she follows me with the air of a stalker as I choose the shoes I am going to wear for the day, funny when she pulls apart a cardboard box with her teeth, throwing the pieces around like confetti; funny when she sniffs the closed box of her favourite crunchy cat biscuits, amazed that, closed up like that, the aphrodisiac smell does not come through; amusing and endearing when, sitting in my lap, she tries to help me read, turning the pages backwards, convinced that this is the best way to carry out such a strange human activity.

Cattus Felix et Ludicus

Albert Schweitzer said, 'There are two ways to escape human misery, playing the organ or watching cats at play'. For Suzy, everything is play.

Not just the chicken drumsticks or the feathers of a pheasant or pigeon, but also the curtains when the wind blows them, a postcard that she slips beneath the door, shadows on the wall that she pursues madly, a pulled thread that disappears into nothing, a soap bubble, the brilliant pearls of an Art Deco abat-jour, the trailing leaves of an ivy, a butterfly zig-zagging through the garden, a feather floating down from who knows where, a rose petal dropping to the ground in autumn.

Happiness, Your Name is Suzy

How could I possibly live now without this little clown in my house, how could I return each evening not knowing that my soft, warm, furry pillow was waiting for me?

How could I give up all the sweet, funny habits that Suzy has picked up over the years?

To rub her tummy as she purrs in happiness that I am home, to unpack the groceries in the kitchen and watch her critically inspect each package, to tease her out of a deep sleep by putting a bit of her favourite cheese under her nose (and then quickly hiding it), to feel her running to hide under the sheets and feel her tremble when there is thunder or heavy rain, to say 'What a lovely concert', when she seems to play the 'cello, inspired by Pablo Casals when licking her back right paw, to take the risk of petting the neighbour's cat knowing how great Suzy's revenge will be (two hours of ostentatious indifference), to go through the house making noises with the scissors or the can-opener (that beloved sound of dinner on its way) to draw out of her hiding place 'that good-for-nothing cat who will really catch it when I find her', thinking up all sorts of excuses to put her in her carrier and take her to the vet, to watch her 'talk' to the pigeons with switching tail, to provoke her into daring, violent games that revive ancestral memories of a ferocious and glorious past, to wait with her for the first crocuses of spring to arrive so that we can both sit outdoors together in the sun.

My dear Suzy, your timid and brave heart, silently passionate and eternally adolescent, is the magic beat of a perfect life, suspended between the stars and the deep blue sea.

You are not a messenger from the devil, nor a good-luck charm nor a *genius loci*, a living tarot, a status symbol or a goddess made flesh.

You are my childhood recaptured, my guide to happiness and my ideal, my small part of the jungle, my partner both sweet and savage, my secret revealed and, as Borges once said about his own Angora, Beppo, the owner of 'a world as closed and separate as a dream'.

CHAPTER XIII
CATS IN PROSE AND POETRY

The Game of Cat and Culture

ALL kinds of cats crawl here and there through the pages of novels, short stories and poetry. Rich and poor, dandies and country bumpkins, fat and scrawny, pagans and angels, skinheads and longhairs, they are often reflections of their owners or the writers who tell of them. They evince the smells, the colours, the emotions and the atmosphere of the book or poem they step through. Below are excerpts from various poems and stories. See if you can guess the title of the work it has been taken from or at least its author.

To check whether you have guessed right, turn to page 96 for a list of the authors and works.

The Ganymede Cat

How splendid you are, Fire . . . I know – because I am Cat – everything that comes with you. I foresee the winter which I embrace with an unquiet soul, but not without pleasure. In its honour, my fur becomes thicker and more beautiful.

My dark stripes turn black, my white chest expands into a splendid *jabot* and the fur on my belly surpasses everything in its beauty.

What cat could resist me? Ah, those winter nights, the serenades under the icy moon, the dignified wait on the rooftop, meeting a rival on a narrow wall! . . . Everything will come about, Fire, just as I tell you. Today the future is opening to the warmth of your new flames. I feel sleepy . . . My purring will stop with your crackling . . . I can still see you and yet already I am dreaming . . . The silky noise of the rain caresses the windows and the gutter sobs like a pigeon. Don't go out while I sleep, oh Fire. Remember that you protect that august rest, that delicate death called, 'the Sleep of a Cat'.

Dr Johnson's Cat, Hodge

I never shall forget the indulgence with which he treated Hodge, his cat; for whom he himself used to go out and buy oysters, lest the servants having that trouble should take a dislike to the poor creature. I am, unluckily, one of those who have an antipathy to a cat, so that I am uneasy when in the room with one; and, I own, I frequently suffered a good deal from the presence of the same Hodge. I recollect him one day scrambling up Dr Johnson's breast, apparently with much satisfaction, while my friend, smiling and half-whistling, rubbed down his back, and pulled him by the tail; and when I observed he was a fine cat, saying, 'Why, yes, Sir, but I have had cats whom I liked better than this'; and then, as if perceiving Hodge to be out of countenance, adding, 'but he is a very fine cat, a very fine cat indeed'.

The Communist Cat

'Comrades', he said, addressing Nino, and Quattro, 'this cat belongs to me. And you want to know what her real name is?'

'Rosella!' Carulina cried triumphantly.

'Eh, thanks a lot!' Giuseppe Secondo said, shrugging haughtily. 'Rosella! that would be her . . . governmental name, you might say . . . less compromising . . . if you follow me. But her real name, the one I gave her when I took her, is different, and I'm the only one who knows it!'

'Doesn't she know it herself?!' Carulina asked, with curiosity.

'No. Not even her!'

'What might this name be?' the two sisters-in-law asked together.

'Tell us! Tell us!' Carulina urged.

'Well, tonight, among ourselves, maybe I can whisper it,' Giuseppe Secondo resolved. And with a conspirator's air, he revealed:

'RUSSIA!'

'Russia! You mean Rosella's real name is Russia?' a sister-in-law asked, not convinced.

'Yes, ma'am. Russia. Yes, indeed.'

Desert Island Cat

. . . when I came back I found no sign of any visitor, only there sat a creature like a wild cat upon one of the chests, which when I came towards it, ran away a little distance, and then stood still; she sat very composed and unconcerned, and looked full in my face, as if she had a mind to be acquainted with me. I presented my gun at her, but as she did not understand it, she was perfectly unconcerned at it, nor did she offer to stir away; upon which I tossed her a bit of biscuit . . . she went to it, smelled of it, and ate it and looked for more, but I thanked her, and could spare no more; so she marched off.

The Fateful Cat

If by good luck there had been an ash-tray handy, if one had not knocked the ash out of the window in default, if things had been a little different from what they were, one would not have seen, presumably, a cat without a tail. The sight of that abrupt and truncated animal padding softly across the quadrangle changed by some fluke of the subconscious intelligence the emotional light for me. It was as if some one had let fall a shade . . . Certainly, as I watched the Manx cat pause in the middle of the lawn as if it too questioned the universe, something seemed lacking, something seemed different. But what . . . ?

The Owl and the Pussy-Cat

The Owl and the Pussy-Cat went to sea
  In a beautiful pea-green boat,
    They took some honey, and plenty of money,
    Wrapped up in a five-pound note.
The Owl looked up to the stars above,
  And sang to a small guitar,
'O lovely Pussy! O Pussy, my love,
'What a beautiful Pussy you are,
    'You are,
    'You are!
'What a beautiful Pussy you are!'

Cat and Lady

They were at play, she and her cat,
And it was marvellous to mark
The white paw and the white hand pat
Each other in the deepening dark.

The stealthy little lady hid
Under her mittens' silken sheath
Her deadly agate nails that thrid
The silk-like dagger points of death.

To a Cat

Mirrors are not more wrapt in silences
nor the arriving dawn more secretive;
you, in the moonlight, are that panther figure
which we can only spy at from a distance.
By the mysterious functioning of some
divine decree, we seek you out in vain;
remoter than the Ganges or the sunset,
yours is the solitude, yours is the secret.
Your back allows the tentative caress
my hand extends. And you have condescended,
since that forever, now oblivion,
to take love from a flattering human hand.
You live in other time, lord of your realm –
a world as closed and separate as dream.

Nothing but Cat

Men wish they were fishes or birds;
the worm would be winged,
the dog is a dispossessed lion;
engineers would be poets;
flies ponder the swallow's prerogative
and poets impersonate flies –
but the cat
intends nothing but cat;
he is cat
from his tail to his chin whiskers:
from his living presumption of mouse
and the darkness, to the gold of his irises.

In my House

I want to have in my house
A sensible woman
A cat walking among my books,
And friends in all seasons,
Without which I cannot live.

The Naming of Cats

The Naming of Cats is a difficult matter,
It isn't just one of your holiday games;
You may think at first I'm as mad as a hatter
When I tell you, a cat must have THREE DIFFERENT
                                    NAMES.
First of all, there's the name that the family use daily,
Such as Peter, Augustus, Alonzo or James,
Such as Victor or Jonathan, George or Bill Bailey –
All of them sensible everyday names.
There are fancier names if you think they sound sweeter,
Some for the gentlemen, some for the dames:
Such as Plato, Admetus, Electra, Demeter –
But all of them sensible everyday names.
But I tell you, a cat needs a name that's particular,
Else how can he keep up his tail perpendicular,
Or spread out his whiskers, or cherish his pride?
Of names of this kind, I can give you a quorum,
Such as Munkustrap, Quaxo, or Coricopat,
Such as Bombalurina, or else Jellylorum –
Names that never belong to more than one cat.
But above and beyond there's still one name left over,
And that is the name that you never will guess;
That name that no human research can discover –
But THE CAT HIMSELF KNOWS, and will never confess.
When you notice a cat in profound meditation,
The reason, I tell you, is always the same:
His mind is engaged in a rapt contemplation
Of the thought, of the thought, of the thought of
                                    his name:
His ineffable effable
Effanineffable
Deep and inscrutable singular Name.

Sources of Excerpts

The Ganymede Cat

Colette, trans Kerry Milis, *Sept Dialogues des Bêtes* (*Creatures Great and Small*)

Dr Johnson's Cat, Hodge

James Boswell *The Life of Samuel Johnson*

The Communist Cat

Elsa Morante, trans William Weaver, *History a Novel* (Sanford J Greenburger)

Desert Island Cat

Daniel Defoe *Robinson Crusoe*

The Fateful Cat

Virginia Woolf *A Room of One's Own* (Harcourt Brace Jovanovich 1929, Leonard Woolf 1957)

The Owl and the Pussy-Cat

Edward Lear, ed Holbrook Jackson, *The Complete Nonsense* (Faber & Faber Ltd)

Cat and Lady

Paul Verlaine, trans Arthur Symons, *Poèmes Saturniens* (*The Book of Cats*, Penguin)

To a Cat

Jorge Luis Borges, 'The Gold of the Tigers' (*The Book of Sand*, Penguin Books 1979, English translation copyright © Alastair Reid 1976, 1977, 1979)

Nothing but Cat

Pablo Neruda, trans Ben Belitta, 'Oda al Gato' (*Selected Poems of Pablo Neruda*, Grove Press)

In my House

Guillaume Apollinaire, trans Kerry Milis, '*Le Poète Assassine*'

The Naming of Cats

T S Eliot *Old Possum's Book of Practical Cats* (Poem reprinted by permission of Faber & Faber Ltd)